The
Name
Game

The
Name
Game

Cultural Modernization & First Names

Jürgen Gerhards

Transaction Publishers
New Brunswick (U.S.A.) and London (U.K.)

Library of Congress Catalog Number: 2005050593
ISBN: 0-7658-0297-X
Printed in the United States of America

Library of Congress Cataloging-in-Publication Data

Gerhards, Jürgen, 1955
    The name game : cultural modernization and first names / Jürgen Gerhards.
        p. cm.
    Includes bibliographical references and index.
    ISBN 0-7658-0297-X (alk. paper)
        1. Names, Personal—German—History. 2. Names, Personal—Germany—History. 3. Names, Personal—Religious aspects—Christianity. 4. German language—Etymology—Names. 5. German language—Gender. I. Title.

CS2541.G46 2005
929.4'4'09430904—dc22

                                                            2005050593

Contents

Foreword

Many individuals and institutions contributed to this study. The collection of data was partly funded by Saxony's Ministry of Arts and Sciences. Mr. Clemens, an official at the registry office in Gerolstein, compiled and computerized the data from the birth register of Gerolstein, a predominantly Catholic town in the Eifel region of Germany between Trier and Cologne. Michael Hölscher collated background information on Gerolstein. Franz Joseph Ferber and Georg Lindenberg helped me to source the photographs that appear in the book. The data on Gerolstein was complemented by a survey of the birth register of the town of Grimma, a small Protestant community near Leipzig. Dorothea Eppler handled the survey and thoroughly investigated and analyzed the texts in the field of name research. In order to decipher the motives underlying parents' choice of first names, Katrin Lieder organized a small survey of post-natal hospital patients in the city of Leipzig. Jan Kaiser compiled the data, classified first names according to cultural groups, and drew up charts. Christian Fröhlich helped to draw up additional charts. I am indebted to Jörg Rössel for his invaluable advice as to methodology and content. To all these I should like to extend my sincere thanks.

Special thanks go to Rolf Hackenbroch, who worked on the project while employed as a research assistant on our faculty (see Gerhards and Hackenbroch 1998; 2000); unfortunately, our original plan to produce a monograph failed to materialize when he left the university to pursue research in the private sector. A fellowship at the Wissenschaftskolleg zu Berlin and at the Swedish Collegium for Advanced Study in the Social Sciences provided me with the ideal environment and bibliographical support to put my ideas down on paper; the stimulating discussions with my co-fellows at both institutes surely left their mark on the book. Last but not least special thanks go to Kevin McAleer, who did not only a terrific job in translating the German manuscript into English, but managed to smooth out the sometimes overly complex German sentences so that they became more easily comprehensible to a general readership.

Berlin
September, 2004

1

Introduction: The Culture of Society

The idea of producing a study of the influence of culture in choosing a first name dates back to an event in 1986. Friends of ours were expecting their first child and were casting about for names. Over food and wine a group of us offered our suggestions. Some were dismissed as too long or too short, others were rejected for being too banal or popular, until finally a name was agreed upon. The criteria governing the selection had not been specified; nonetheless, it was clear to me as an observer that the search process was subject to a structuring principle not solely determined by the individual preferences of the parents-to-be, but which conformed to a logic directly related to the couple's social status and milieu. Both parents were university graduates whose cultural capital included more than a passing acquaintance with music, literature, and art, thus enabling them to express their taste in a way both acceptable to their social peers and in a way that clearly distinguished them from other milieus. The repertoire of potential first names was thus confined to those acceptable to the parents' social milieu. Names from films, television, and sports were judged to be vulgar, since they were often used by the lower classes. Old German names like Wilhelm, Uta or Otto were rejected on grounds of being too traditional and otherwise conservative. Jewish names like Sarah or Daniel would have been considered if they hadn't been used a decade earlier by the same milieu; they were shopworn and did not satisfy the parents' need to christen their child with something distinctive and individual. The name finally decided upon was Stella.

Let me relate another experience. A few months ago, my two children (Niklas and Hannah) celebrated their birthday with friends. The guests were Maurice, Leon, Anselm, Julius, Lea, Laura, Sarah, Katharina, Jamie, Annabelle, and Henriette. But what had happened

1

to Heinrich, Otto, Josef, Wilhelm, Berta, Erna, Maria, Annegret, and Elizabeth? These names would definitely have cropped up at a birthday party, say in the 1930s. First names have undergone a profound change since then. Erstwhile favorites are now "out." Names from German-Christian culture are perceived as old fashioned and have been replaced by newfangled ones. This shift is neither arbitrary nor erratic but conforms to patterns that can be posited as social rules.

The social and cultural structures determining the choice of first names is the subject of the present study, but at the same time it will hopefully offer an introduction to cultural sociology. Culture as a category of research has boomed since the "cultural turn" sparked off a revival of cultural sociology in the social sciences and humanities. However, I do not find the premises underlying the "cultural turn" and its implications for research in the area of sociology persuasive. Based on the example of first names, I shall attempt to show that the classic tools of sociology and its scientific-theoretical logic are more than adequate for investigating the culture of a society. I will use classic theories of cultural modernization and try to show which theories and methods can be applied in analyzing cultural change. Based on an analysis of names, I shall attempt to demonstrate a specific interpretation of cultural sociology and explain what characterizes this interpretation.

The "Cultural Turn" and the Problems It Raises

Scholarly interest in "culture" is at an all-time high. In the past fifteen years cultural studies have become a separate discipline, new research foci have developed, and whole faculties have been renamed cultural studies faculties. The various disciplines have undergone a reorientation (for historical studies see Daniel 2001). These institutional and intellectual reshufflings were instigated by a flood of publications endorsing just such a reorientation (for the humanities see articles in Frühwald et al. 1991). These trends have also had an impact on sociology. In 1988, Jeffrey Alexander summed up the theoretical trends in sociology and spoke of the "cultural turn" that had occurred in the social sciences (Alexander 1988).[1] Despite its complex and heterogeneous nature, the "cultural turn" has certain distinguishing traits, very clearly summarized by Andreas Reckwitz (Reckwitz 2000: 15). I will discuss each of them separately.

1. Scientific theory and epistemology are concerned with how knowledge in general and how scientific knowledge in particular is acquired. According to scholars promoting the cultural turn, theories of science were previously based on a mirror theory of knowledge: something out there in the world that can be described and explained by an independent scientific observer. In a critical analysis of this perspective, the "cultural turn" has shown that no category-free observation of the world is possible and that scientific findings are strongly influenced by the categories one uses. The existence of scientific categories is itself a result of a social process that can be depicted through a sociology of knowledge and science. I find three aspects of this premise of the "cultural turn" and the consequent implications for scientific practice debatable. (1) The fact that scientific findings are always category-dependent is by no means a new insight of the "cultural turn." It had, ironically, been earlier elaborated by advocates of critical rationalism who are now under siege from the "cultural turn." Only naive empiricists claim that the world can be experienced directly. Statements about the world are statements by subjects who make statements. In discussing the problem of fundamental principles, Karl Popper and others stressed that every science is based on fundamental principles which can be presumed valid if the scientific community as a whole agrees to them.[2] In critical rationalism the criterion of objectivity is thus replaced by the criterion of intersubjectivity. "Logically speaking, the testing of a theory can be traced back to basic propositions which are defined as fixed first principles....The empirical basis of science is not absolute. Science is built on marshy land, not solid ground" (Popper 1976: 73, 75). (2) Yet Karl Popper and other critical rationalists do not conclude from the relativity of scientific knowledge that scientific knowledge is arbitrary. Science is the consistent attempt to approach the truth (approximation theory of truth). The logical testing of the consistency of assertions, the disclosure of their underlying operative assumptions, and the precise use of definitions are tools used to achieve this approximate truth. Some scholars of the "cultural turn" draw another practical conclusion from the basic relativity of scientific knowledge which I also find unconvincing. They interpret the relativity of scientific knowledge as an invitation to ignore many "standard" criteria of scientific research; hence the assumptions upon which their studies are based are often insufficiently explained, the terms fuzzy, and the statements rarely empiri-

cally tested. (3) The fundamental dependence of scientific knowledge on categories still does not imply that this has any significant impact on concrete research. The path from scientific assumptions to concrete research topics is usually a long one, and general premises are only reflected to a limited degree in specific research (see Alexander 1987). This merely indirect link between general scientific principles and concrete empirical research is often ignored by scientific theorists. If, say, we are interested in whether and when the first names of monarchs and princes are adopted by the masses and we empirically analyze this based on the diffusion of princes' names following coronation, then I do not see what kind of fundamental scientific assumptions need here be taken into consideration.

2. The focus of every sociological analysis is to reveal the meanings behind a person's actions. The meanings of actions are not simply the idiosyncratic, subjective meanings of one acting subject, but are the result of interactions with other people and have the status of collective-meaning systems, world images, ideas, codes, schemata, symbolic orders - in a word, they have the status of culture. Proponents of the "cultural turn" claim to have introduced the importance of culture and meaning as a challenge to a mechanistic concept of human behavior and society. This second idea is not bulletproof either. It is correct, of course, to assert that human beings use meaning to define their relationship to the world, and insofar as sociology examines the meaning-systems that underlie our actions it is indeed of a cultural bent. But is this really a novel insight? Do any sociologists deny it? Even Émile Durkheim, often accused of being a positivist, perceived man as a creature whose actions were founded on meaning, as we will shortly see. And even rational-choice theories start from the assumption that people choose actions based on their *definition* of situations and not on the basis of objective facts, and that "frames" shape and limit their behavior (see Esser 1991). Ergo, it is hard to resist the idea that the "scientific counterposition" criticized by advocates of the "cultural turn" is itself their own construct. Of course the rise in German names from the nineteenth century onward cannot be interpreted as a mechanistic phenomenon. The development is linked to the rise of nationalism in Germany as a collective-meaning system; and the decline of a transcendent interpretation of the world (secularization) is reflected in the decline in Christian names. An analysis of first names is always concerned with the meanings inhering to those names.

3. Because sociology must take the meaning of behavior into account, advocates of the "cultural turn" have attempted to limit sociology's competence. They say that sociology—in contrast to the natural sciences—is not in a position to formulate and test hypotheses. According to the "cultural turn," cultural-sociological analysis consists solely in understanding the subjective meaning of an action on its own specific terms. I'm not persuaded that sociology must limit itself to an interpretive description of social phenomena, it should do this and more. Following a description of the *explanadum*, the second step should be to explain (*explanans*) the thing described. The fact that we are dealing with meanings should pose no obstacle. Rainer Schnell, Paul Hill, and Elke Esser (1995a: 91) have given a lucid example of this:

> In bar A, person X notices person Y smiling at them, whereupon X approaches Y, invites Y to a beer, etc. In fact, Y's smile does not "mechanically" move X to action in a way similar to a rise in temperature creating an increase in gas volume, but rather the "smiling" gesture is perhaps interpreted as a sign that Y likes X and would enjoy a conversation. This interpretation is a prerequisite for X's going over to meet Y. Moreover, it is not just a single symbol but a number of interpreted symbols that generate X's subjective judgment of the situation. A smile in a late-night bar is different from a malicious smile of a colleague at work after some blunder by X. The same gesture has a different meaning in different situations. In the social context there is also the possibility that symbols, situations and/or milieus have become relatively consolidated and thus are not liable to ever-changing interpretations or (as constantly stressed by the symbolic interactionists) the possibility and necessity of new interpretations of symbols. This latter of course is also liable to a deductive-nomological explanation, for the question as to why X interprets the smile of Y as a sign of being liked can be answered through the *explanadum* of a learning theory. And such is still basically explicable despite the fact that intended meanings and their imputations are never fully identical. These divergencies call forth various theoretical *explanada* attempting to make sense of them, as is done in socio-linguistics. (Schnell, Hill, Esser 1995a: 91)

4. The "cultural turn" led to a shift in focus, micro-sociological analyses of everyday phenomena and practices now coming to the fore. Analyses of the creation of meaning in everyday situations is of course not an inevitable result of the first three premises of the "cultural turn," but it reveals such a tendency. As Karin Knorr Cetina stated in 1988, social reality must be analyzed "from the native's point of view," and if one follows this dictum then very soon we find ourselves analyzing everyday practices. The analysis of organizations concentrates less on their formal structures than on the informal quotidian routines of *members* of organizations and the organizational cultures that emerges therefrom; the traditional class analysis is replaced by "cultural studies" that chiefly depict the ev-

eryday routines of the lower orders. Phenomena such as gratitude, shame, passion, and honor thus become objects of cultural-sociological analysis—namely, the description of society as a symbolic practice of its constituent members (Knorr Cetina 1988).

There are no *scientific* criteria, which can be used to decide whether a research question is a meaningful one or not. So, one cannot really criticize the fact that cultural sociology focuses so much on the study of everyday life phenomena. One can merely draw attention to the gaps that emerge when cultural sociology concentrates solely on an analysis of daily life: it misses the larger macrosociological connections. A purely micro-based cultural sociology cannot precisely answer the question as to what a society's culture is. The classic cultural sociologists were interested in the exposition and explication of macro-cultures, for example, people like Max Weber in his work on " The Protestant Ethic and the Spirit of Capitalism" and "Western Rationalism." With my analysis of first names I will employ the everyday perspective of the newer cultural sociology, while combining it with a macro-sociological approach. The naming of children as an everyday societal occurrence will be interpreted as an indicator of both macro-cultural change and a process of cultural modernization.

5. Implicit in the "cultural turn" is a criticism of standard scholarly methods and a preference for so-called qualitative methods of social research. The basis for this preference is emphasis on the cultural aspect and the meaning dimension of social actions. The "cultural turn" argument is that standard quantitative methods are unable to capture the meaning of actions and interactions; they treat the objects of their research as a world free of meaning (Reckwitz 2000: 27); it is important in empirical analyses to "qualitatively" describe the meanings of human actions. But is this portrayal of quantitative methods and its accompanying critique correct and legitimate? I disagree with the notion that so-called quantitative methods neglect the meaning dimension. The difference between quantitative and qualitative methods is not that one depicts meaning and the other does not; the difference lies in when and how they do it. In quantitative methods the meaning of a person's attitude in a survey or the meaning of a person's statement in a newspaper is defined *before* the data is collected albeit on the basis of a preliminary examination. If, for example, one agrees, in a survey, with the statement that Jews are more corrupt than other people, then this will be

taken as an indicator that the respondent holds an anti-Semitic attitude. In qualitative methods the meaning of words is reconstructed *after* the data has been collected, for example, in an open-ended interview. But both approaches are concerned with sniffing out meaning, and the quantitative methods used here in my analysis of first names will hopefully illustrate that fact. For instance, if parents give their children names of Christian saints then the implicit *meaning* is that they are expressing their Christian faith; when this practice wanes over time, then I interpret it as a sign of increasing secularization in society. The categories saintly names/other names, in fact, first *emerge* through attribution of meaning—namely the interpretation of the abandonment of saintly names as an indicator of social secularization. Of course, one can challenge the notion that a decrease in saintly names is indeed an indicator of secularization processes—although one would have to put forth some very cogent arguments. What seems to me indisputable, however, is that this approach is concerned with meaning. Every quantitative approach is to some degree a qualitative one (see Früh 1992). This of course does not mean that there are no differences between qualitative and quantitative methods and that qualitative approaches do not have their place. The choice of which method one uses depends on what one wishes to ascertain. If, as in this study, one is doing an analysis of cultural change and is working at the macro-level, then one must take care that one's material is representative of the whole of society. This approach perforce has a greater affinity to quantitative methods, that is, controlled random sampling that makes it possible to infer from the sample to the entire population.

To sum up: I, for one, remain skeptical of the "cultural turn" in sociology. One can still employ the classic premises of sociology to work up cultural-sociological questions and answer them empirically, and I would like now to elaborate my own understanding of cultural sociology by discussing the work of Émile Durkheim.

Back to Durkheim: Concepts of Cultural Sociology

In 1895 Émile Durkheim published *The Rules of Sociological Method* in which he developed his ideas for a science of society. Two years later came his study *Suicide*, which was intended to demonstrate the methodologies laid out in the prior book. The texts went hand in hand (Lukes 1973: 226) and helped establish sociology as an autonomous discipline. The principles behind Durkheim's understanding of science in general and his notion of sociology in particular can be reduced to six basic rules: (1) write simply and plainly; (2) define your terms as precisely as possible; (3) make no assertion regarding the real world without funding it on empirical evidence; (4) always examine the plausibility of alternative views and explanations that stand in contradiction to your own theories; (5) the sociologist's proper subject is human behavior or actions (by which he meant not those of individuals but of a number of individuals who act in the same way); (6) explain human actions within their social context.

Suicide exemplifies Durkheim's ideas. Not only is the text simply written but Durkheim takes the reader through his argument on a careful step-by-step basis. His terms are precisely defined and empirically grounded. With the help of official statistics from various countries and regions, he attempts to back his assertions of socially determined suicide rates empirically and then prove them through the method of concomitant variations.[3] Alternative explanations are extensively discussed and proofed. Above all, Durkheim attempts to refute psychological and physiological explanations of suicide rates and thus create a genuine sociological perspective that does not try to explain individual suicide but rather suicide *rates* (collective behavior). Durkheim attempts to make sense of suicide rates through various social factors—religious ideas and their organizational forms, family structures, state integration, etc.—and thereby establish suicide as a social product and a relevant object of sociological study. And finally, insofar as only a portion of behavior variance can be traced back to social context, Durkheim is not attempting to show that social conditions determine individual behavior but only that they point to certain likelihoods.

Durkheim has been criticized as being a positivist and a collectivist (Aron 1979: 58). The reproach of positivism is largely the result of his unhappy choice of the term "social fact." But this term was not intended to imply that the objects of sociological investigation are not fundamentally different from those of the natural sciences. It is precisely in *Suicide* that Durkheim is at pains to show that unlike the objects of natural science research, sociological objects are cultural phenomena vested with meaning. He explains the higher suicide rate of Protestants in relation to Catholics by looking at the ideational content of both religions: "The Protestant's faith is more largely a self-creation. He takes his Bible in hand and no interpretation is forced on him. This religious individualism is a characteristic feature of Protestantism....We are thus able to conclude that the susceptibility of Protestantism for suicide is connected with this religion's spirit of self-determination and free inquiry" (Durkheim 1983: 169). Raymond Aron nicely summarized Durkheim's understanding of a social fact:

> Durkheim's treatment of the objects of sociological study as facts is perfectly justifiable if you understand facts to mean every reality whose outside form can and must be observable but whose nature is not immediately recognizable. On the other hand, if the word "fact" means that the sociological object allows for no other interpretation than that of a natural object or if sociology should deny any human meaning to the object in question, then his interpretation is wrong. Such an interpretation, however, would contradict Durkheim's very own method, for in all his works he attempted to discover what sort of meaning individuals and groups attached to their lifestyles and beliefs and rituals. What he called understanding was grasping the inner meaning of social phenomena. An interpretation of Durkheim's thesis in moderated form simply implies that this authentic meaning is not readily apparent but must be discovered and revealed. (Aron 1979: 59)

More persuasive is the accusation of collectivism, which has been most strongly leveled by the school of methodological individualism. Similar to Durkheim, James S. Coleman concedes that, "The main task of social science lies in explaining social phenomena, not in explaining the behavior of single individuals" (1995: 2). But Coleman and methodological individualism chooses a divergent path to this shared goal, via explanations of individual behavior that go to forming an aggregate social phenomenon. And it is precisely this step—from the micro to the macro level—that remains so underexposed in Durkheim (see Lindenberg's [1983] criticism). He makes connections between certain collective phenomena and other collective phenomena, for example, religion (Protestantism/Catholicism) and suicide rates (high/low) without explicating how macro factors *structure* human behavior and how an aggregate phenomenon like suicide rates can *emerge* from individual human behavior. An explicit and complete explanation would necessarily assume the structure of a bathtub, as sketched by Coleman (see Coleman 1995: 10).

Insofar as Durkheim's sociological goal was—among others—to explain the correlation between religions and suicide rates, it was imperative that he (1) describes the effect of different religions on the believer's definition of meaning then (2) explicates the relationship between the believers definition of meaning and their behavior, and finally (3) shows how the actions of individuals impact the suicide rate, which he does through the simple process of addition. The accusation of collectivism is certainly legitimate when one sees how Durkheim fails to bathe in the "tub" of a micro/macro explanation. At the same time, one should note that Durkheim operates *implicitly* with such an explanation. In the course of my own study we will be confronted with this problem of a complete explanation often enough.

My fascination with Durkheim's suicide study rests not solely on the formal stringency of a genuine sociological argument but also with the study's content—that very aspect captured my imagination as a young student. I was struck by Durkheim's choice of suicide as a vehicle for conveying the viability of sociology as an explanatory mode. Although suicide seems to be a highly idiosyncratic phenomenon dependent largely on personal decisions and the "psycho-logic" of individual cases, Durkheim succeeds in showing that there are certain patterns one can trace using empirical data based on suicides that have taken place under similar social conditions.

I have been at pains to describe not only the theories underlying *Suicide* but its concept of self-annihilation as a sociological phenomenon, because these have strongly influenced my own views concerning sociology and form the background to my analysis of names. In this analysis I shall attempt to follow the Durkheimian dicta by using a plain and simple language, by being precise in my definition of terms, and by funding my theoretical assertions with empirical evidence. Additionally, I am not so much interested in the question of individual names as in the composite trends these display at certain points in history, and then to explain them by way of their social context. Moreover the object of my study has parallels with Durkheim's suicide study: not only one's departure from life but one's formal entrance into it—both matters of a seemingly private nature—are socially structured.

Every newborn in Germany receives one or more first names that must be reported to the registry office. The newborn's first and surnames together encapsulate his identity for all those with whom he has any dealings. Names generally mark a person for life: if someone calls his name he reacts to it, his name often becomes synonymous with his own individual characteristics, and it will evoke certain images originally associated with the bearer. But a name is also a source of identity *for* its bearer. In the course of one's socialization a person develops a certain relationship to his name, attributing characteristics to it that have been won through self-knowledge as well as the observations of others. We remember the feeling of neglect we had as schoolchildren when a teacher called us by the wrong name; and the teacher likely felt a moment of shame at having committed such a gaffe. One's identity is closely tied to one's name. For this reason, name-changes and name mix-ups can serve in altering one's identity. Sects and other "total institutions" use this strategy to distance members from their earlier social context and identification markers, subsequently bestowing upon them new ones.

In contrast to last names, first names are selected. As a rule it is the parents, sometimes in consultation with relatives and friends, who decide from among the myriad possibilities. This unhindered choice of the parents would appear to bespeak little if any outside social influence. But can one still formulate suppositions and hypotheses that make plausible such social influence? To what degree does the cultural context affect this seemingly private decision? If such hypotheses can be empirically funded then they would indeed illustrate how society impacts on even the most private of sectors, thus demonstrating the explanatory power of cultural sociology. Succinctly put, this study is primarily concerned with showing how first names are socially contingent.

This analysis has not been conceived solely as a contribution to the limited field of name research; its goal is more ambitious. First names and the changes they have undergone in the last hundred years will serve here as an indicator of the process of cultural change. Indicators, of course, are empirical "symptoms" that point to the existence of hypothesized facts; they stand for "something" without being that "something" themselves. I will be using the development of first names above all as an indicator for measuring the processes of cultural change. I am going here on the assumption that macrocultural developments are reflected, as it were, in the micro-phenomenon of first names, and in my study I describe these processes and explain their causality.

In this aspect too I am following the ideas of Durkheim. His main goal was not to explain suicide rates in and of themselves. Suicide rates were for him an indicator for measuring the integrative force of societies in general and that of modern societies in particular. Durkheim understood the modernization process as undermining traditional interpretive authorities. Hence he reads the Reformation as the dissolution of the interpretive monopoly of the Catholic Church and the birth of individual religions that set the secularization process in motion. Durkheim sees the higher suicide rates of Protestants in relation to Catholics as being only a further indication of the diminishing relevance of religious interpretations in the modern world. His view of the development of the family and the state is similar, their bonds having been loosened over time, and he cites as evidence the high suicide rate among single adults and childless couples as well as in states during peacetime rather than in times of war.

My goal is to use first names as a heuristic for describing processes of cultural modernization in the last hundred years. I am taking my lead from cultural indicator research as developed by people like Georg Gerbner and Karl Erik Rosengren (Gerbner 1969; 1973; Rosengren 1981; 1986; 1989; Melischek/Rosengren/Stappers 1984; Namenwirth/Weber 1987).[4] Cultural indicator research differs from survey research in that this latter does not possess the data to examine long-term developments. Content analysis of documents is the only practicable means by which to observe long-term processes of cultural change.

What are first names symptomatic or symbolic of? Or put more technically, which theoretical constructs can be "measured" using first names? To reiterate, I am here investigating the development of first names from the end of the nineteenth century to the end of the twentieth, using their development as an indicator of cultural change and using theoretical constructs that are largely classic in nature.

In the past, *religion* formed one of the central authorities for interpreting everyday phenomena. Consequently, after explicating in chapter 2 the data and methods to be employed in this study, I will begin chapter three with an analysis of the influence of religion on first names that will be theoretically spearheaded by the notion of greater secularization. To what extent are Christian names displaced by other types of name? Is this process similar for Catholics and Protestants? How can one explain the process of increasing secularization?

In chapter 4 I will analyze the development of German names over the last hundred years. Our main concern here will be the impact of different *political regimes* (Second Empire, Weimar Republic, Third Reich, West Germany, East Germany) and the accompanying rise and fall of nationalist sentiment on German names. How were first names affected by the rise of nationalism in the nineteenth century and its hyperbolic climax in Hitler, and then by the subsequent disrepute into which nationalism fell after 1945?

Family and relations form the third traditional means of integration and imparting meaning. Many scholars perceive the decreasing significance of kith and kin as one of the central aspects of cultural modernization. The dissolution of the family as a unit of production and the growing importance of work and a career outside the household—revealed statistically in a shrinking of the primary sector— made for less familial obligations and ties. In chapter 5 I will investigate to what degree this process was reflected in first names and ask, as I do in every chapter, how they might be explained.

Religion, nationalism, family and relations form the traditional matrix for imparting meaning and structuring behavior. If these reference points become fragile and lose their significance—then what? Ralf Dahrendorf sees the loosening of traditional ties as an absolute prerequisite for liberating the individual personality, Ulrich Beck and Georg Simmel attest to such a development, and Beck perceives a relationship between greater *individuation* and the *blurring of class distinctions*. In chapter 6 I will consider whether there were similar processes at work in the area of first names.

The decreased significance of both the German and Christian cultural spheres allowed for the penetration of previously foreign names, a phenomenon which I will analyze in chapter seven and describe as a process of *globalization*, or, more precisely, as a process of transnationalization; the new and previously foreign names were hardly "global" in scope, but were limited to certain select cultures. In this same chapter I will describe how after traditional cultural ties were loosened first names took on a life of their own and became largely matters of fashion. What were the dynamics of these certain fashions and what was the logic behind a name making the top-ten list?

The various processes of cultural modernization treated in the respective chapters are symbiotic in nature: the dissolution of religious, national and familial ties enabled the liberation of the individual personality and subsequent processes of individuation and globalization.[5]

In the eighth chapter I will discuss gender-specific aspects of first names. To what extent are personal appellations used to delineate the sex of a person and can we ascertain any social change over time with regard to a decrease in such gender-specific names? Do parents restrict themselves to a certain pool of names depending on their child's sex and are these bound up with gender-specific roles? Has this changed in the past hundred years?

The ninth and concluding chapter will draw up a balance sheet.

Notes

1. Paul Rabinow and William M. Sullivan (1979) spoke some years earlier of an "interpretative turn." The various positions within the German social sciences are clearly presented in a collection published by Holger Sievert and Andreas Reckwitz (1999).
2. It therefore makes little sense to denounce Popper as a positivist.
3. "We dispose of a single means by which to ascertain if one phenomenon is the cause of another: comparing those cases in which both phenomena appear or are lacking and then investigating whether the variations that they exhibit under diverse conditions prove that one phenomenon is dependent on another. If the observer believes the phenomena could be otherwise produced, then here we have the experimental method per se. On the other hand, if production of the fact is not subject to any arbitrariness and can only be brought into a cause-and-effect relationship with the other phenomenon, then this is the indirect experimental or comparative method" (Durkheim 1976: 205).
4. A research group led by Karl Erik Rosengren in the Swedish research program CISSS attempted to do a historical and synchronic study of Sweden's culture. For instance, Eva Block (1984) depicted the change in meaning of values such as freedom and equality in Swedish culture through an analysis of lead articles in five leading Swedish dailies. Karl-Wilhelm Grümer and Robert Helmrich (1994), Jürgen Gerhards and Astrid Melzer (1996) tried to portray secularization processes through analyses of German obituaries.
5. Heiner Meulemann (1993) and Jan Peters, Albert Felling and P. Scheepers (1993) illustrated how the various hallmarks of cultural modernization are not only theoretically but empirically intermeshed. Peter Ester, Loek Halman and Ruud de Moor (1993) and Ronald Inglehart (1989) sketched out the causal relationship between structural processes of modernization (technological and economic factors) on the one hand and cultural modernization processes on the other.

2

Data, Methods, and Research Context

Data Base and Methods

The empirical findings of this study are based primarily on a representative sampling of names from the birth registry offices of two towns in Germany, Gerolstein and Grimma. But this is no local study. Which raises the question: From such a study *can* one draw larger conclusions that might apply to all of Germany? Statistical science replies in the negative because births in Gerolstein and Grimma are not a random sample of births throughout Germany. So does this mean that the validity of my study's findings is restricted to the two towns from whence they were derived? I say no—and for the following reason.

Whenever possible I have factored in research findings from other regions of Germany and compared them with those from Gerolstein and Grimma. Additionally, I have tested them against the data assembled by Michael Simon in his painstaking research on the development of first names in three areas of Westphalia—the city of Münster, the town of Versmoldt, and the village of Ostbevern (1989). Using parish registers, he compared the structures and changes in first names in these three communities from the seventeenth century to 1980, and in his appendix he documented all the names appearing in the three communities at certain points in time. I constructed a data set from this source and was able to draw comparisons with Simon in answering some—unfortunately not all—of my research questions. This comparative approach, using not only the Simon study but others, helped to regulate my results. As it turned out, the trends I discovered from the late nineteenth to the late twentieth century were extraordinarily similar to trends I found in other data sets. Thus I saw fit to encompass Germany as a whole in the results of my study, and not just restrict them to the two towns in question.

From Gerolstein, I studied information pertaining to the first hundred registered births every four years between 1894 and 1950 and then every two years between 1950 and 1994; for Grimma it was the first 100 births every two years from 1894 to 1998. The data's categorization consisted of the following variables: date of birth, first name,[7] and sex of the child; and the religion, profession, and first names of both father and mother. The Gerolstein data was computed by a registrar (and supplemented with other variables), and a student assistant Dorothea Eppler handled the Grimma data. I have classified the first names of children and their parents according to their cultural origins and was aided in this regard by two name handbooks (Droskowski 1974, Gerr 1985). Many names have undergone transformations, for example Katharina is of Greek origin (adapted from the female name Aikateriné) and then became Christianized with Saint Katharina of Alexandria. Martin is of Latin provenance (referring to Mars, the god of war) and during the Middle Ages gained a foothold in the Christian world via Saint Martin of Tours. In such cases I have recognized the name's most recent convolution, proceeding from the hypothesis that this was more relevant to parents, i.e., that parents naming their children Katharina or Martin were identifying with Saint Katharina or Saint Martin rather than with the name's Greek or Latin genesis.

For classifying the parental professions I have used a system adapted from that of Ralf Bohrhardt and Wolfgang Voges (1995) and that of Hans-Peter Blossfeld (1985), this latter having been developed for use in various educational studies at the Max Planck Institute.

An analysis of birth registries allowed me to check our hypotheses regarding the naming process, the names themselves functioning as macro-trend indicators. This, of course, provides little insight into the motives of parents in their choice of names. As a supplement to the birth registries, therefore, we interviewed mothers in hospital delivery rooms in order to learn their reasons for the choice of a certain first name and to see if (present-day) subjects were aware or unaware of the cultural factors influencing their choices.

How are the social structures of Grimma and Gerolstein constituted and how have they changed over time? Gerolstein is a town in the Eifel region of western Germany, some one hundred kilometers from Cologne,[8] and is primarily Catholic. In 1995, 82 percent of its inhabitants were Catholic, 10 percent were Protestant, and 7 percent had another faith or none at all. Until the late nineteenth century, Gerolstein and environs was something of a backward area. It was far from any major urban centers, was inaccessible by any rivers or railroads or paved roads, had poor soil and climate for farming, and enjoyed few mineral resources (see Doering-Manteuffel 1995). This situation first began to change with the building of the railway line between Cologne and Trier in 1871. The national railway became an important employer for denizens of the region, enabled commutes to urban centers on the Rhine and in the Ruhr Valley, and stimulated the development of a metal industry (wire manufacturing) and the establishment of the Gerolsteiner mineral springs. The wire factory Christian Oos was founded in 1882, the Flora Mineral Spring in 1883, and Gerolsteiner Mineral Water in 1888. Further railway lines to Prüm and to Mayen/Koblenz improved communications and trade and enabled the establishment of more industries with Gerolstein becoming a small commercial and transport center in an area dominated by agriculture and suffering from a lack of infrastructure. Gerolstein's late economic development in comparison to other regions impacted its demographic and social-structural development. Its population increased from 950 in 1895 to 1,564 in 1905, and to 3,050 by the end of the 1930s. At the same time, the percentage of the population engaged in agriculture slowly receded. In 1909, a petition for establishing a secondary boy's school was forwarded because the town had achieved a central position in the Eifel region and it was feared that employees of the railway and the postal service would leave if they saw no prospect of their children receiving an adequate education (see Nowatschin 1986: 133). While the Gerolstein population worked—and still works—mainly in the service sector and for the large enterprise of Gerolsteiner Mineralbrunnen, villagers in the surrounding community were active in the agrarian sector. Gerolstein has a hospital that services an area some twenty kilometers wide, so that mothers of babies who are not necessarily part of the Gerolstein community proper are still registered with the Gerolstein registry office. Today the city itself has about 7,500 residents, its surrounding community some 15,000.

Grimma is a town located in eastern Germany, from 1949 to 1990 part of the GDR. The social structure and development of Grimma is much different from that of Gerolstein (for the following, see Stadtverwaltung Grimma 1999). Inhabitants were mainly Protestant, but after 1949 they were increasingly without any official religious affiliation. In the late nineteenth century, Grimma was an agrarian town, but citizen income also came through skilled trades. In addition, Grimma was a military and bureaucratic center, with a population of 9,769 in 1895, and by 1900 it boasted ten schools. Grimma was already a well-known educational center in 1550 when the third Saxon regional school was housed there in a former monastery to prepare students for the university at Leipzig (see Teiche, Naumann and Schwalbe 1999). In 1799, Göschen moved his publishing house and printing press from Leipzig to Grimma, and in 1813 he issued the town's first newspaper. Grimma had been a garrison town ever since 1663 (see Teiche 1999) and in 1819, after the Wars of Liberation against Napoleon, a hussar regiment of 1,065 men was stationed there. Grimma was also an army town in the GDR and remained so until Soviet troops withdrew in 1993. Industrialization came to Grimma relatively late (Teiche 1999a). In 1867, Henschel established a mechanical engineering works that numbered 300 employees in 1900, and there were also glove and stationery factories. This engineering works tradition was preserved through the twentieth century and received fresh impetus from the GDR regime when VEB MAG was given the main state contract for chemical processing, thus expanding the city through larger residential areas and consequently increasing the population. Today Grimma has 18,000 inhabitants.

Research Context

Sociologists and historians have some times used first names as a cultural indicator. Some works (Miller 1927; Rossi 1965; Taylor 1974; Lieberson 1984; Alford 1988; Lieberson and Bell 1992; London and Morgan 1994; Lieberson and Mikelson 1995) do attempt to reconstruct class, gender, and ethnic differences in the selection and innovation of names. Streiff-Fenart (1990) has analysed names of children of mixed French-Magrebian couples as an indicator of successful cultural reproduction. Watkins and London (1994) compare the patterns of personal names of Italian and Jewish immigrants and native-born whites to describe the transformation of social identity and the process of assimilation. The most interesting examinations of the diffusion of names through the class structure are the works of Taylor (1974) and of Lieberson and Bell (1992). Few studies can be found which have analysed first names as an indicator of cultural change. Most of the studies done by historians deal with earlier time periods (Main 1996; Smith 1985). Weitman (1987) has analysed first names given to children in Israel between 1882 and 1980 as an indicator for national and ethnic orientation. There is a rich French literature on the change of personal names during the last two hundred years (Besnard 1995). Dupaquier et al. (1987) have analysed first names during the nineteenth century; Besnard and Desplanques (1986) have analysed first names in France from 1890 to 1985 and Besnard and Grange (1993) focus on first names and the polarization of social taste. As Besnard (1995) points out, the main focus of these different French studies is to analyze the existence of class differences in taste and the influence of the vertical diffusion of tastes. This also is one of our topics, but unlike these studies our research is more theory driven and tries to analyze cultural modernization in a broader way.

Two recently published studies of first names should be mentioned separately. Michael Wolfsohn and Thomas Brechenmacher (1999) have analysed the development of first names for the last two hundred years in different regions of Germany. The focus of their research lies on the question, how different political regimes and especially the names of the representatives of different political regimes have influenced the process of name giving of the broader public. The two authors interpret the process of taking over the names of the leaders of a political regime by the people as an indicator of the legitimacy of the political regime. The second study comes from Stanley Lieberson (2000). Lieberson's book is the best study dealing with first names from a sociological perspective. His ideas and methodological considerations have inspired the following chapters a lot. I will refer to and discuss his hypothesis and empirical results in the different chapters.

Notes

1.   Until 1976, in the case of there being more than one first name, the name by which the child was to be called was underlined, and I have treated this as a first name. After 1976 there was no designation of the name by which the child was to be called, but based on the experience of registrars, one can generally assume that parents entered the name by which the child was to be called as the first name.

2.   Most of the following information has been taken from a volume on Gerolstein issued by the city itself (see Stadt Gerolstein 1986).

3

Secularization Processes and the Dissolution of Religious Ties

Secularization Processes

Religion was and is a central aspect of the culture of society and thus a main concern of cultural sociology insofar as religion's ideational systems exercise a major influence on the actions of the humans embedded in such systems. The influence of religion on the actions of humans can be seen not only in matters directly relating to religion, such as prayer and church attendance, but finds its expression in extra-religious behavior that can manifest itself in bellicose conflicts or terrorist assassinations or in even less spectacular ways such as political elections or economic activity. In this chapter, I will explore the effects of religion on first names, and because we are primarily interested in processes of cultural change we will be inquiring as to the *changing* influence of religion on first names.

For the theoretical description of the changing influence of religion there is the concept known as *secularization*. The word comes from the Latin word *saeculum*, which had the original meaning "gender," then later, in the figurative sense, "generation" and "world epoch." "Increased worldliness" seems to be the most accurate etymological rendering of secularization. The social sciences designate secularization as being the changes adopted by modern societies at various levels (see Lübbe 1965, Luckman 1980, Zabel 1984). Peter L. Berger defines secularization as the "process through which parts of society and segments of culture are freed from the domination of religious institutions and symbols." (Berger 1973: 103). Berger distinguishes three aspects. (1) Social-institutional secularization is the institutional separation of church and society in general, and church and state in particular. This found its first historical expression in the

Reformation and its secularization of church holdings, the abolition of monasteries and convents, and the expropriation of their lands by secular agents. This process found its sequel in the increasing autonomy of "various segments of the social structure" from normative religious tutelage (Luckmann 1980: 168). (2) Cultural secularization is a change in the central pattern of attitudes and value systems in Europe beginning with the Enlightenment, namely the decreasing importance of religious views of nature and society. From Karl Marx's work critical of religion to Wilhelm Dilthey's writings on Western intellectual history, from the religious-sociological studies of Ernst Troeltsch and Max Weber to the cultural-sociological work of Friedrich H. Tenbruck—cultural secularization has been regarded as a central element of modern culture. Cultural secularization, however, encompasses not only the dissolution of a transcendental interpretive model but its replacement by worldly alternatives. It has largely been science that has replaced the interpretive power of the church, banishing the Gods, bringing heaven down to earth, and thereby contributing to the "demystification of the world" (see Weber 1988: 564). A hallmark of modern culture is the preponderant role played by science (see Tenbruck 1989: 126-42). (3) Finally, Berger speaks of a subjective dimension to secularization. This concerns the consciousness of the individual citizen and proceeds from the idea that an increasing number of people can manage quite well without any religious interpretations at all.

Berger's three aspects of secularization are helpful insofar as they permit a more accurate placement of our analysis within the framework of the debate. We are investigating processes of subjective secularization to the extent that we are charting how frequently parents choose first names that have religious relevance. Of course, the term subjective secularization is somewhat inappropriate due to its implicit assumption that the subjective decision is independent of the cultural matrix in which the individual is necessarily embedded. I therefore prefer the term subjective-cultural secularization because it makes clear that we are dealing with individual decisions duly informed by their cultural context.

Before we turn to our analysis proper, it is perhaps advisable to examine the recent debate over the use of the secularization concept. There is disagreement as to whether and to what degree there have indeed been any secularization processes—in the sense of subjective-cultural secularization—in the development of Western industrial societies (see the overview in Wohlrab-Sahr 2001). There are chiefly two research findings that questioned the idea that modernization processes are tied up with those of secularization. Recent American economic-religious sociological work shows that in the USA, one of the world's most advanced countries economically, membership in religious organizations and participation in their activities have not diminished but rather increased over time (see Stark 2000, Finke and Stark 1992). This finding casts serious doubt on the thesis that modernization processes automatically lead to secularization.

The secularization thesis has also come under fire from another quarter. Thomas Luckmann (1991) holds that because religion has simply changed from a visible to an invisible faith, there has been no accompanying subjective secularization process. "Social structure is secularized, but not the individual" (Luckmann 1980: 172). While visible religion is characterized by reference to established religious forms, the new religiosity is distinguished either by private forms or through a rise in civil religion. One can observe an increase in religious and civil religious movements that have succeeded in establishing themselves outside of the large official church structure and in gaining adherents to their faith. These two objections regarding the secularization hypothesis are helpful insofar as they can refine one's own analysis and limit overly bold assertions. Let us first look at American religious development.

American religiosity teaches us that one must specify the conditions under which secularization processes can take place. This is made particularly clear in Rodney Stark's (2000) explanation for differing patterns of religious development in Germany and America. Stark criticizes the secularization hypothesis for spending too much time analyzing changes in the so-called demand side of religion. Economic welfare, a rise in educational levels and the increased role of science in shaping worldviews does not automatically mean a diminishing role for religion in people's lives. Stark formulates an economic theory of religious development that is first and foremost concerned with supply-side structures. According to him, the German religious market is distinguished by an oligopoly consisting of two official churches that are financed through a church tax collected by the state and whose clergy draw salaries as de facto state officials. Moreover, this oligopoly has been successful in hindering the establishment of other faiths, which have been systematically defamed by the two official churches and supported in this by the state. This structure has been firmly in place for centuries, with the result that there has never been a free market competition for believers. There is no stimulus for the two established churches to do much tending of their respective flocks, to win new membership, and pursue the work of conversion. Consequently, there has been a growing apathy among the faithful toward their church and its offerings.

The situation is entirely different in America. Here there are a total of 1,500 denominations that are financed through donations and not through a state-supervised church tax; the establishment of new churches and the attainment of a tax-free status is a simple one and publicly legitimized. The survival of individual churches is directly dependent on their success in recruiting and retaining members. The competitive structure has led to an increase rather than a decrease in religiosity in the USA.

What are the consequences of Rodney Stark's economic theory and his findings for our analysis? The "supply-side" analyses and interpretations of the development of religiosity do not principally contradict the "demand-side" secularization hypothesis; they do however make clear that secularization is possible only under certain conditions. Social-structural changes—mostly described using modernization concepts—only lead to conditions conducive to secularization if they are not impeded by a supply-side competition for religious membership. One must therefore add the proviso *ceteris paribus* when formulating hypotheses regarding secularization within the context of the religious marketplace. In view of Stark's work, it makes sense to include in any analysis more than just the general social-structural framework that influences people; one should analyze the actors—in this case the churches—and their actions and influence with regard to secularization processes. We will take up these considerations when we investigate the difference between Protestant and Catholic communities.

As already mentioned, Thomas Luckmann asserts that there have never been any real secularization processes at work, simply an increase in civil-religious offerings and a development of the religious toward pluralism and privatization. This thesis is very much conditioned by Luckmann's understanding of religion. He defines religion as an anthropological constant of human existence resulting from the fact, that only man has self-consciousness (Luckmann 1980: 176). As creatures who *must* attribute meaning to their lives and who are able to reflect on their past, the present and the future and who also know that they will die, humans are, perforce, religious animals. Luckmann concludes therefore that there is no human life and society without religion (see Luckmann 1980: 177). Thus, a subjective-cultural secularization in the sense of a lessening of religiosity is by definition impossible.

My notion of religion is—compared to Lukmann's definition of religion—a more restricted one. When we speak of religion we are speaking of a view of life and the world based on the existence of a higher transcendent reality. The difference between immanence and transcendence is at the core of any religion. (see Eliade 1957). "In its most general (sociological) meaning, religion is a bond or orientation of humans (mostly groups) directed toward a final and/or otherwordly reality" (Homann 1994: 261). This general definition varies only in the specifics of the transcendental interpretations imposed by the respective religions. For instance, at the center of the Christian interpretation is the notion of an omnipotent God, creator of nature and man, a God who gives meaning to human existence. The entire structure of nature, with the earth as focal point and humans as the crown of creation (only humans can communicate with God, God became Man), is interpreted as a divinely created order. The history of mankind thus acquires its specific teleological sense: it begins with the expulsion from Paradise and ends with the Last Judgment and the possibility of once more achieving Paradise. Despite the temporal nature of human existence, death does not end in nothingness but is a passage into a potentially better life and thus loses its fearful aspect of finality (see Nassehi and Weber 1989: 108). All immanent events have meaning derived from a specific transcendental understanding.

If one defines the essence of religion as a belief in transcendence, then the essence of any secularization process would be the dissolution of transcendental views. Cultural secularization thus means the breaking up of religious, in particular Christian, frames of reference. One can speak of cultural secularization when there is a diminution of transcendental understandings of one's earthly existence. One can expect—and here we recall Rodney Stark's findings—that under conditions of a religious oligopoly with two institutionalized churches one can observe processes of secularization.

What does secularization mean in terms of first names? The "hereafter" aspect of first names is their affiliation with Christian saints, the nucleus of which is the martyrs, persons who gave their lives for their faith (see Bieritz 1991). After the martyrs come the semi-martyrs, those who may not have died but who suffered torture and persecution for their faith. Important bishops and theologians form a third group, and ascetics and virgins a fourth (see Bierritz 1991: 218f). Worship of the martyr saints, of these blood witnesses to Christ, took place on the anniversary of their death. People gathered at the grave of the saint and recited his or her passion, and they celebrated the *passa christi*—Jesus' resurrection from the dead and ascension into heaven. The anniversary of the martyr's death was also celebrated as a day of rebirth. The saints served two purposes. On the one hand, they were models to be emulated (*imitatio*) in terms of their religious self-sacrifice; on the other, they could be called upon (*invocatio*) to provide intercession with God. With the waning of the Middle Ages, the second purpose emerged as much the dominant one.

First names of saints also had this double function.[1] The saint was a model of behavior and, far more important he was a transcendent patron and mediator with God. The link between the saint and the child bearing his or her name was established through the christening, then renewed on a yearly basis by celebrating the saint's feast day—identical with the anniversary of that saint's death. Hence, we can speak of a secularization process when there occurs a dip in the percentage of names of Christian origin.[2]

Figure 3.1
Percentage of Christian Names (1894-1994)

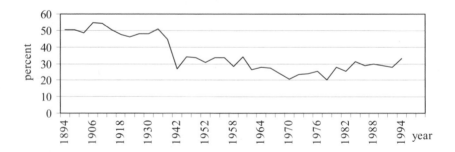

Figure 3.1 shows the percentage of Christian first names over a century. From 1894-1994 the percentage of Christian first names dropped from 50 percent to 32 percent. This constitutes a dramatic change. Increasingly unimportant is the transcendent function of Christian names as conduits to God via a patron saint. In 1894, Katharina, Anna, Maria, Magdalena, and Elisabeth were among the most common names for girls; in 1994, Katharina, Laura, Sarah, Julia, and Michelle were typical. The empirical results thus support the secularization thesis. But the trajectory is not a gradual one. From 1934-1942 there was a big secularization spurt that we will examine in greater detail later. Furthermore, after 1980 the percentage of Christian first names rose—something which we will also be taking a closer look at when we investigate fashion trends. But this much can be said: after 1980 Christian names had been denuded of their Christian meaning and were rather in sync with the trend of new names, that is, the trend of resuscitating old ones.

What might be the reasons for the process of secularization? Secularization processes are frequently explained—both theoretically and empirically—by pointing to modernization trends (see Jagodzinski 1995; Jagodzinski and Dobbelaere 1995). Two factors play a unique role: the development of economic and life-sustaining conditions, and advances in education.

The thesis that there is a causal nexus between educational developments and secularization tendencies had already been adumbrated by Émile Durkheim in the connections he drew between education and Protestantism in his suicide study (1983: 177). Education raises the likelihood of self-examination and an informed worldview. With increasing education there is an increased chance that tradition will not be taken at face value but rather questioned with regard to its functionality and possibly even broken with—according to the hypothesis. Public education changed in the course of the twentieth century in three respects: it became accessible to larger segments of the population, the illiteracy rate being reduced to negligible levels; it grew ever longer in duration; and a greater total percentage of the population now attained higher education. For example, the percentage of university students increased enormously from the beginning of the twentieth century. In 1872, ten of every 10,000 German males were university students; 1912 = 21; 1950 = 26; 1960 = 45; 1970 = 69; 1982 = 154 (see Hohorts, Kocka and Ritter 1975: 161; Petzina, Abelshauser and Faust 1978: 169; Rytelewski and Opp de Hipt 1987: 220). We can assume that such increases negatively influenced the willingness of people to follow religious teachings, and first names over this period do in fact reveal the lessening influence of Christian tradition.

According to modernization theory, the second factor having an impact on the process of secularization is the conditions determining quality of life. This theory stems from the religious sociology of Karl Marx and Friedrich Engels who incorporated the religious ideas of Friedrich Feuerbach. The growth and persistence of religion is explained in terms of earthly factors: "All religion is nothing more than the phantasmagoric reflection in people's minds of those external powers that rule their daily existence, a reflection in which the earthly powers assume the form of heavenly ones" (Engels 1973: 294). "Phantasmagoric products" such as religion are perceived by Marx and Engels as compensation for the trials and vicissitudes that people undergo in their lives. These trials are of a double nature. They consist on the one hand of the constant threat posed by nature, by things such as plague and flood; on the other, they consist of social impediments, above all the economic conditions of survival.[3] In order to endure the burdens imposed by nature and society, humans invented religion. Religion has a supernatural interpretation of this earthly veil of tears: "Religious misery is at one and the same time the expression of real misery and a protest action against it. Religion is the sigh of the burdened creature, the soul of a heartless world, just as it is the mind of mindless conditions. It is the opium of the masses. True happiness will only emerge when the illusory happiness of religion is eradicated" (Marx 1972: 378).

With this last remark, Marx is indicating the preconditions under which religion will lose its power and persuasiveness: as earthly happiness waxes, the need for religion wanes. By earthly happiness, Marx mainly means the securing of living conditions and economic welfare. One can derive from this presumed link a hypothesis: the less existential and material need—that is, the greater prosperity—the less need there is for religiosity. Twentieth-century developments do indeed indicate an improvement in living conditions. This is manifested in what Arthur E. Imhof (1994) terms "the newly-won years" and "the better years." Life expectancy has dramatically increased in the past century and a half. Average German life expectancy went from 37.2 years in 1855 to 74.6 years in 1985—a doubling in an extremely short period of time (see Imhof 1994). (The causes of this dramatic improvement were many and cannot be individually discussed here—see Imhof 1994: 67). The extra years were also better years. For one, during the period under investigation, the German social system was developed. The percentage of people who received welfare and had pensions and medical insurance continually rose. In this way, the social state mitigated the principal risks of human existence (we will undertake a closer examination of the relevant empirical findings in our chapter on the diminishing role of the family). Secondly, the average weekly and yearly workload was reduced and leisure time subsequently increased. Arthur E. Imhof (1994: 82) has calculated not only average life spans for 1900, 1980, and 2000, but the time people in these years spent engaged in "life-essential time" (including such activities as sleeping, eating, drinking, and hygiene), "work time," and "free time." His findings were that the percentage of free time had increased dramatically: "The rise in free time from 110,000 hours in 1900 (25 percent of one's lifetime) to 280,000 hours in 1980 (46 percent) and 370,000 hours in the future (53 percent) rests in large part on the shrinkage in work time. In 1900, it made up 34 percent of one's lifetime budget, whereas in 1980 it was 12 percent. In the future it will likely be no more than 6 percent per day, per week, per year and in the course of a lifetime. We have more leisure time during our working life as well as more years for retirement (Imhof 1994: 83).

Finally, the disposable income of people in the twentieth century increased, raising individual economic welfare. It is, however, difficult to ascertain exactly how high these income increases were. One finds statistical information for 1871-1914 regarding the average real annual earnings (income related to the cost-of-living index) of employees in industry, trade and transport (Hohorst, Kocka, Ritter 1975: 107). The real average earnings rose 78.5 percent from 1871 to 1913. The information concerning subsequent periods is not wholly comparable. For the period 1913/14-1944 there is empirical data regarding the real wages of workers as measured by the cost-of-living index (Petzina, Abelshauser and Faust 1978: 98). Real wages during this period increased 13.9 percent (1913/14-93; 1944-106). For the period 1950-1980 one can likewise discern an increase in the real wages of industrial workers (Rytlewski and Opp de Hipt 1987: 119). With 1976 equaling 100, 1950 was 31.4 and 1980 was 108.6, making for an overall increase of 245 percent. One can presume that income increases for other occupational groupings were similar in the period 1870-1980 (see Pierenkemper 1987), meaning that incomes rose fourfold.

In general, we can see the modernization process as one in which there was increasing security in terms of basic living conditions and a rise in prosperity and leisure time. One can presume that this process had a negative effect on religious attachments and thus contributed to secularization.[4] This general secularization process is also reflected in a secularization of first names.

But modernization theories alone cannot explain the decrease in Christian first names over time. As figure 3.1 showed, the secularization process does not describe a smooth path. Between 1934 and 1942 there was an intensive phase of secularization. In the next chapter we will see that during this same period German names increased, a development that can be traced to the influence of National Socialism (see Gerhards and Melzer 1996). A political regime's attitude toward religion establishes the costs and incentives of religious faith among its citizenry and in turn impacts secularization processes. Political regimes such as National Socialism that successfully limit religious freedom and/or offer alternative ideological systems help to accelerate secularization processes (see Berger 1973: 106), liberal regimes will have a neutral effect, and regimes with religious affinities will tend to impede secularization processes.

National Socialism was an anti-clerical regime that simultaneously offered a German-nationalist ideology acceptable to a substantial portion of the population. Kurt Nowak (1995) has shown that National Socialism managed in several ways to bring about a distinct lowering in the level of religious culture and church affiliation: through the replacement of denominational schools with *Gemeinschaftsschulen*, through pressure on parents to keep their children from taking religious instruction, through the formation of Hitler Youth and *Bund Deutscher Mädchen* (girl's counterpart to the Hitler Youth), cells to compete with the religious youth groups, and through harassment of religious societies and the setting up of rival National Socialist organizations. The battle waged between National Socialist ideology and Christian belief systems showed itself in numerous ways in everyday life.

In the photo on next page—taken on 1 May 1939 in Pelm, a village pertaining to the district of Gerolstein—one sees swastikas and a crucifix peacefully coexisting.[5]

By contrast, the next two photographs illustrate the head-to-head competition between religion and National Socialism. While before 1933 the representation of Christian symbols in the classroom was normal—here the crucifix and the Virgin Mary—a few years later these symbols have been replaced by a photo of Adolf Hitler. One finds a similar shift in first names, the Christian names being replaced by German ones.[6]

National Socialist success in the construction of a German tradition and history was tremendous, and, with the growth in German first names as an indicator, penetrated deep into the family starting in 1934. The fact that secularization processes can be accelerated by political regimes is supported by findings of political sociology, which can be summarized under the catchphrase, "bringing the state back in" (see Skocpol 1979 and Evans, Rueschemeyer and Skocpol 1985). These findings refute generalized social trends, instead positing the specific influence of states on social and cultural developments.

To sum up: Over the course of the twentieth century one can clearly discern secularization processes at work in the naming of children. The percentage of Christian names—from the Bible and those of saints—declined. Secularization was the result of two factors: 1. Modernization processes that noticeably improved people's security and welfare and raised their educational levels, thus reducing their reliance on religion and increasing their skepticism toward "God-given" structures; and 2. the partial ouster of Christian worldviews through National Socialist ideology. The limited scope of our analysis does not allow for a strict empirical testing of the causal relatedness of secularization, modernization, National Socialist

ideology and the establishment of an anti-clerical regime; but taken together their plausibility and explanatory power seems to be evident.

Protestants and Catholics

Until now I have not divided my analysis of the process of secularization processes into Protestant and Catholic. But not only do the ideational content and the church politics of the two religions differ, they are also at variance in the area of first names. The divergence was present from the start—in the Reformation. European first names began to grow more and more "Christian" as of the tenth and eleventh centuries when people began naming their children after saints (Kohlheim 1996). This process dovetailed with the increasing veneration of saints and saintly relics, every church as well as every guild and social caste having its own patron saint. In the late medieval era the veneration of saints and their relics and the increase in pilgrimages and indulgences assumed such proportions that "it had more in common with magic and superstition than with religion" (Hausberger 1994: 653).

The Reformation was a violent break with tradition when it came to saintly veneration and first names. The Lutheran form of Protestantism was primarily opposed to the monopoly on salvation exercised by the medieval Catholic Church. It was believed that every individual received grace through faith. One's individual relationship to Christ was determinant, while the church in its role as go-between with God was of only secondary importance. This theological reorientation implied a criticism of the Catholic Church's hierarchical organization, of the sacrament of confession, of indulgences, and numerous other practices and rituals. By contrast, Protestantism emphasized individual responsibility and the necessity of a personal and unmediated relationship to Holy Writ because the word of God was regarded as sole source of revelation. In addition, Protestantism showed a marked preference for an ecclesiastical structure that was less hierarchical and which had as its fundament the individual autonomous churches whose leadership partly consisted of laypersons. With its basic principle of *solus Christus et sola fide*, the Reformation likewise brought about a change in attitude toward the veneration of saints—a great distaste for which had originally inspired Luther to refocus Christian faith on the Bible and Jesus Christ. He roundly condemned the invocation of saints as being a superstitious practice: "Appeal to the saints is an abuse and violates the main article of faith and obscures one's witness to Christ. It is neither necessary nor advisable, has no basis in scripture, and one can do a thousand times better by turning directly to Christ" (cited in Schulz 1994: 665). In the final analysis, the Bible recognizes only a single holy figure—Christ. From this perspective, the appealing to saints is tantamount to a denial of Christ's exclusive mediating role. Luther thought that the traditional veneration of saints distracted from essential faith.

The Protestant view of the veneration of saints is contained in the Augsburg Confession, composed by Philipp Melanchthon and read before the Holy Roman Emperor Charles V and the Augsburg Reichstag on 25 June 1530. It consists of twenty-eight articles, the first twenty elaborating the teachings of Martin Luther and the remaining seven addressing abuses of the Catholic Church. Article 21 concerns the veneration of saints: "We teach that saints have efficacy in that one may strengthen one's faith in pondering the grace that was theirs and how they were helped through faith; moreover, one should take their good works as an example in one's own calling....But one cannot find anywhere in Holy Scripture where it says that one should appeal to the saints or ask for their assistance. 'For there is one God, and there is one mediator between God and men, the man Jesus Christ'" (First Letter of Paul to Timothy 2,5).

At a minimum, the Reformation laid the theoretical groundwork for a change in first names among Protestants. It is debatable to what degree and at what rate this theological shakeup actually influenced Protestant first names. Volker Kohlheim reports that on the heels of the Reformation, names in Protestant areas did change; Biblical names increased and those of saints became rarer (Kohlheim 1996: 1054). By contrast, Christian Grethlein emphasizes how the Reformation was a turning point that initially failed to turn with regard to names, having a real discernible effect starting only in the mid-eighteenth century (Grethlein 1996: 756).

The Catholic Church responded to the Reformation with the Counter-Reformation, and that in a very concrete fashion regarding the veneration of saints and their use as namesakes. At the Council of Trent in 1563 the *"Decretum de invocatione, veneratione et reliquiis Sanctorum, et sacris imaginibus"* was promulgated. It rejected the Protestant claim that the veneration of saints contradicted the Word of God and detracted from His worship. The Council determined that it was good and efficacious to make humble appeal to the saints and beseech their aid in enlisting God's help (see Hausberger 1994: 654). In the *Catechismus Romanus* of 1566 it said: "Finally the child to be baptized receives a Christian name. It should be the name of a saint who, through his outstanding piety and fear of God, has done honor to the altar. This kinship of names will be a mild spur to the child to emulate the virtue and holiness of his namesake. And as it strives to imitate him, it should also pray to him and trustingly expect his protection of body and soul. One must therefore rebuke those who christen their children with the pagan names of degenerate people—likely a sign of how little an upright Christian life is esteemed in those places where reigns such pleasure in these disreputable figures that they allow unholy names to constantly profane Christian ears" (Gatterer 1941: 70). The tradition by which one named a child after saints was not only continued and strengthened, but it became prescriptive behavior for all Catholic faithful.

This spiritual control was structurally based on a strong integration of Catholic believers in the Church and the interpenetration of the Church with everyday life. This applied above all to the period in which our study is situated—the nineteenth century—a period in which the Catholic Church developed in two directions. First, the Pope succeeded in consolidating the centralized structure of the church and fortifying his own authority. The goal of this ecclesiastical strategy was to throw up an impregnable dam against the modern and secular deluge (Wehler 1995: 387). At the same time, there was a new and powerful surge in Catholic piety among the populace. Participation in village processions and the feast days of patron saints increased; everywhere new Catholic societies were established and the various monastic and priestly orders grew in membership. This rise in popular piety continued after 1871 (Wehler 1995: 1189) and (particularly in the countryside) led to a greater integration of the populace with Catholic-Christian practice.

So we see here the differences between the two denominations with respect to first names as well as their theological-ideological and practical-institutional differences. Accordingly, one might expect secularization processes to have taken place in completely different ways vis-à-vis first names. Figure 3.2 shows the percentage of Christian names for the Protestant community of Grimma and the Catholic one of Gerolstein.

Here our theoretical expectations are indeed met. By the end of the nineteenth century the percentage of Christian first names in Catholic Gerolstein was around 70 percent, whereas in Protestant Grimma it was about 40 percent. The Reformation's split between popular Catholic piety and the veneration of saints on the one hand and a worldly Protestant ideology on the other showed itself unmistakably in the sphere of names. Both communities witnessed a downward trend in the percentage of Christian first names that continued until about 1980. Until that date both religious communities experienced a secularization process—more pronounced and dynamic in the Catholic case. The secularization spurt after

Figure 3.2
Percentage of Christian Names

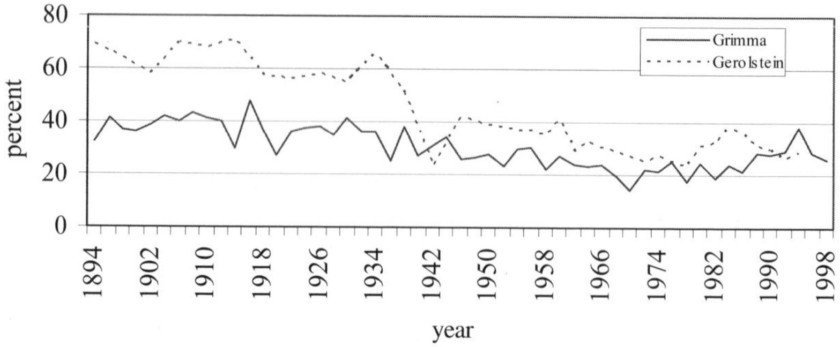

1934 was due to the increase of German names during this period, which I will elaborate in the next chapter.

Gerolstein and Grimma are both small-town communities. Michael Simon's data allows us to focus our findings: it is safe to assume that religious integration in the countryside was greater than in the cities. This has partly to do with the countryside's lower level of modernization—also expressed in its higher percentage of people occupied in the agrarian sector—and partly to do with the fact that ecclesiastical control of religiosity is easier in a relatively homogeneous rural community than in a heterogeneous city. One therefore presumes that secularization processes in cities take effect earlier than in the countryside, and this is confirmed when comparing the percentage rate of Christian first names in the Catholic city of Münster with the percentage rate of Christian names in the Catholic rural community of Ostbevern. The percentage of Christian first names in Münster is about 12 percent less than in Ostbevern (dates not given).

But let us return to Christian first names in the Catholic community of Gerolstein and the Protestant community of Grimma. The differences between the two religions begs caution in formulating general secularization hypotheses that fail to take into account the specific cultural orientation and behavior of those supply-side providers of religion—the argument made by American sociologists of religion. The basis for the different cultural orientations influencing first names was first laid in the Reformation. The Protestant church emphasizes the importance of a direct human relationship to God without any mediating institutions; it is solely through the Bible that man can build a relationship with God. Accordingly, Émile Durkheim called Protestantism the first individualistic religion. Protestant criticism of the Catholic Church's go-between function stems from this idea of a direct relationship to God, and its rejection of the veneration of saints is a component part of this criticism, issuing in the commandment: Thou shalt not name children after saints. The Counter-Reformation responded to this by strongly encouraging the use of saints' names. These two contradistinctive imperatives did much to effect the difference in names which would emerge between the Protestant and Catholic communities in years to come.

But Reformation and Counter-Reformation do not fully explain these differences. For in the lapse of time between the Reformation and 1894 (starting point of our data), Christian first names in Protestant and Catholic areas had varying trajectories. This cannot be shown with our own data, but we can analyze Michael Simon's church-register data, thereby allowing us to place our twentieth-century findings in a larger historical continuum.

Figure 3.3
The Percentage of Christian Names in a Catholic and in a
Protestant Community (1780-1900)

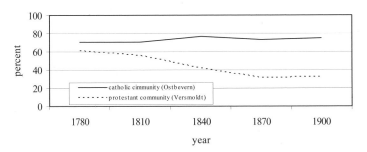

In comparing the two trajectories, one sees that the secularization process was hardly a linear development. While the percentage of Christian first names in the Catholic community from 1780-1900 rose by a few percentage points,[7] during the same period the percentage of Christian first names in the Protestant community tailed off dramatically. Starting in 1900 (as shown in the previous diagram) secularization in both communities proceeded at the same rate, if at different levels.

As mentioned, the percentage rate of Protestant names cannot be traced back solely to cultural groundwork laid by the Reformation and Counter-Reformation, for these predated eventual Protestant rejection of Christian first names by one or two centuries. One must also take into consideration the specific politics of the Protestant Church from the late eighteenth to the twentieth century. During this period the Protestant church gradually merged its authority with that of the state and formed a close association with Prussia that by the end of the nineteenth century had resulted in a fusion of Protestant doctrine and nationalism that went by the name of National Protestantism (*Nationalprotestantismus*). This process was also visible in the increase of German first names at the expense of Christian ones, which we will analyze in the next chapter.

In this chapter we have seen that in the course of the twentieth century there was a distinct secularization of first names. The percentage of Christian first names with their origin in the Bible or in the names of saints decreased. This phenomenon is owing to the concatenation of several factors. For one, modernization processes dramatically improved people's welfare, security, and education and accordingly reduced the "demand" for religious orientation while increasing criticism of "God-given" laws. Simultaneously, in order to grasp secularization processes one must take into account the worldviews and strategies of the supply-side providers of religion. The differences between Protestants and Catholics in the sphere of first names can only be explained if one also compasses the varying theologies emerging from the Reformation and Counter-Reformation as well as Protestant and Catholic Church politics. Lastly, the drop-off in Christian first names after 1933 shows that any explanation must factor in not only the offerings of supply-side providers but the additional strategies of competing secular interpretations: the precipitous decline in Christian first names after 1933 was obviously a byproduct of National Socialist ideology, which succeeded in persuading people to choose ethnic German rather than Christian first names for their children.

Notes

1. The mediating function of saints between the earthly world and the hereafter was not only relevant to first names, individual castes, professional groups, countries and locales also had their own saints.
2. A further indicator of secularization and individuation processes would seem to be the fact that today only the birthday of a child and not their saint's feast day is celebrated.

3.   These economic conditions are of course determined by the ownership of the means of production and the class struggle, but I am leaving that aside here in order to focus on Marxian religious sociology.

4.   Wolfgang Jagodzinski (1995) has been able to establish this connection through a comparative study of the "German Länder."

5.   The photo is courtesy of Fritz Klasen.

6.   The first photo is courtesy of Margot Haring from Wassertiesch, the second photo by kind permission of Norbert Ledner from Morbach.

7.   The original impetus behind the increase in Christian first names was owing to the strengthening of piety among the populace (see Sperber 1984) something we will discuss in greater detail in the next chapter.

4

Regime Change and the Rise and Fall of German Names in the Twentieth Century

Kurt, Ernst, Friedrich, Heinrich, Karl, Hermann, Otto, and Wilhelm are typical German names for men. Edeltraud, Ulrike, Friederike, Sieglinde, Dörte, Margit, and Gisela are popular German names for women. In the previous chapter examining Christian first names, I made repeated reference to German names. As our classifications according to cultural origin together total 100 percent, the increase in names from one cultural milieu means a decrease in names from other cultural milieus. If one combines German and Christian names, then it becomes clear that the German and Christian cultural milieus formed the two traditional ligatures for first names. Figure 4.1 shows the percentage of German and Christian names over time.

Figure 4.1
Lessening Influence of Tradition
(Percentage of German and Christian Names)

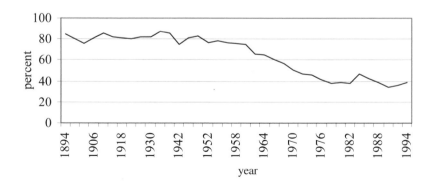

At the end of the nineteenth century, about 85 percent of names given children were German or Christian. Names from other cultures such as the French or Anglo-Saxon played a negligible role in terms of numbers. Names were thus largely restricted to the two traditional (and closed) cultural milieus. This high percentage of Christian and German names remained relatively stable up until the establishment of the Federal Republic of Germany and the German Democratic Republic. This then changed very rapidly as Germany opened itself to the outside world after the Second World War and Germans increasingly availed themselves of names from other cultures. We will examine which precisely these foreign names were in chapter 7.

Figure 4.2
Percentage of German Names (1894-1994)

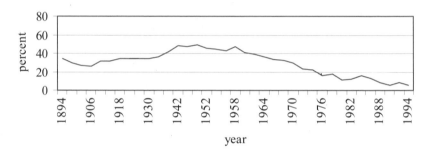

After a slight dip at the turn of the century, the percentage of German names rose from 30 percent to 50 percent following the Second World War and establishment of East and West Germany in 1949, only to then decrease continually in significance until 1994 when it sunk to around 5 percent. The rise in percentage of German names at the beginning of the century is earmarked in particular by a rapid increase during the 1933-1942 period.

Before we analyze the reasons for this development, we should once more place German names in their historical context. Our own data begin in 1894, but as mentioned, we have also adapted Michael Simon's data on names in three Westphalian locales so as to place our own analysis along a larger historical continuum. In so doing, one sees that the increase in German names was already underway by the start of the nineteenth century. This increase continued until the First World War and then rose sharply in the succeeding period, only to level off again with the establishment of the two German

states. The increase in German names was not a phenomenon instigated by the Nazi regime but had a long prehistory in the nineteenth
century, thus giving an indication of its possible causes.

Figure 4.3
Percentage of German Names (1810-1980)

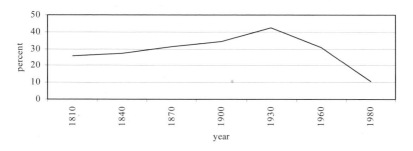

The increase in German names was obviously a consequence of
German national development. "A political nation arises with the
formation of national consciousness within the populace. We perceive this process as an increase in collective political consciousness, whereby members of a certain ethnic group and/or inhabitants
of a certain territory discover that they have common traditions and
interests" (Dann 1996: 14). We will not here go into the various
phases of the nineteenth-century formation of German national consciousness but merely say that in its first phase (late eighteenth century to early nineteenth century) nationalism was principally a movement among the intellectuals and other elites, and grew to become a
mass phenomenon only in the 1820s.[1] The widespread associational
life in Germany at the time with its university dueling clubs (e.g.,
Burschenschaften), gymnastic clubs (*Turnvereine*) and choral societies (*Sängerschaften*) increasingly won large sections of the population over to the idea of a German nation. National meetings and
festivals, national literature and theater helped mobilize people for
the nation and generated a feeling of commonality, even if this had
yet to be translated into the idea of a shared political nation (Breuilly
1999). The definitions of "commonality," however, could be quite
varied. The idea of *Volksnation* was a community of similar ethnic
extraction; *Kulturnation* meant a community with a shared language
and other cultural traditions; the integrating force of *Staatsnation*
lay in its consolidation of citizenry under the ruling power of the
state (Wehler 1995: 938-46).

With the founding of the German Empire in 1871, German nationalism was radicalized and politicized. As of this date, the political conditions were present for the idea of the German *Volksnation* and *Kulturnation* to merge and synthesize and culminate in an imperial German nationalism (Wehler 1995: 938-46). The choral societies and gymnastics clubs and shooting clubs regarded the Prussian-dominated German Empire as their nation-state. The Franco-Prussian War (1870-71) was the constitutive act, and the victory at Sedan was thereafter celebrated as a national holiday. The army was seen as the school of the new nation, and the prolific formation of *Kriegsvereine* (war societies) and erection of war memorials served as its symbols (Dann 1996: 186).

Historians have shown that German nationalism was characterized by a preponderance of ideas relating to *Volksnation* and *Kulturnation* and remained untethered to any notion of a shared constitution. It was precisely this indifference that made German nationalism relatively compatible with whatever political system, be it the Kaiserreich, the Weimar Republic, or the Third Reich (Wehler 1995: 952). With the First World War, nationalism experienced a further escalation. Even such groups as the German Social Democrats—who had always been very skeptical of nationalism—were swept up in the nationalistic fervor, unanimously authorizing the declaration of war and the voting war credits.

The construction of a nation to a large extent also includes the construction of a common history and past. An ex post teleological interpretation is imposed on the status quo, which is perceived as the result of an inevitable historical process. According to Hans-Ulrich Wehler, the Borussian school of historical writing (Droysen, Mommsen, Sybel et al.) fancied Prussia to be the integrating force of an emerging German nation, and this Borussian school had a far-reaching influence beyond scholarly circles. Accompanying the creation of a German national consciousness were histories of "great men" who were seen as leading figures in strengthening the nation. "From Hermann the Teuton to Karl the Great [Charlemagne], from Luther to Friedrich the Great, their progress was styled as a predestined development that found its final fulfillment in German unification in 1871, in the new empire, and in Bismarck's achievements (Wehler 1995: 951).[2]

The names of figures designated as forefathers of German history were precisely those considered to be exemplary names for newborns. This trend extended from the nineteenth century to 1949, and its continuity can be seen in the percentage of German names in figures 4.2 and 4.3 (see also Wolffsohn and Brechenmacher 1999).

As in other areas, National Socialism seized upon this tradition and took it to extremes. The goal was to nationalize the masses through propaganda and determined buildup of an organizational structure that pervaded all levels of society—and this goal was duly achieved. The concept of the nation was funded by *volksnational* and racist ideas that excluded other nations and peoples. The success of the Nazi's German-national ideology can be seen in the potent rise in German names as of 1933. The way to this development had been cleared by processes that had their beginnings in the nineteenth century, and especially since the First World War. National Socialism had an effect on names not only by generating a German-national climate that caused parents to choose from among a limited pool of names, but through concrete political measures. In a decree of 14 April 1937, it was required that "German ethnic comrades" call each other by German names (see Grethlein 1994: 757). Those in need of orientation could find it in advice manuals (Fahrnkrog 1939). In a 1938 law Jews were still allowed to use Jewish names, but all Jewish men with German first names were required to add "Israel" to it and all Jewish women with German first names had to attach "Sara" so as to be clearly identified as Jews (see Grethlein 1994: 757). But Jewish names had been stigmatized long before. Dietz Bering (1992) demonstrates this in his study of official name-change applications by Jews, examining the names most frequently changed ("escape names") and the preferred alternatives ("target names") (see also Beck-Gernsheim 2002).

The percentage of Jewish-Hebrew names in Grimma and Gerolstein is not especially high, so I have aggregated the various points in time into different time-intervals figure 4.4 shows the percentage of these type names over time.

Just as the upward trend in German names did not first begin under National Socialism, the decrease in Jewish-Hebrew names had already set in much earlier and continued into the 1960s. The upswing in Jewish names thereafter was owing to the fashionableness of names from previously alien cultural milieus, parents with professional degrees tending more than others to give their children Jewish-Hebrew names. We will analyze this in greater detail later on.

Figure 4.4
Percentage of Jewish-Hebrew Names

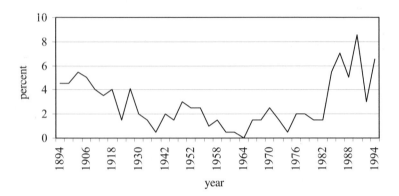

Thus we may interpret the rise in German names as well as the downward trend in Jewish names as the result of a nationalism that had been gaining ground ever since the start of the nineteenth century and had experienced peaks with the establishment of the Kaiserreich in 1871, the First World War, and the National Socialist takeover, thereby defining and structuring the choice of first names. Nationalism and the construction of a German tradition and history obviously reached into the most private corners of family life—thus causing the rapid increase in German names.

The lost war and the fall of National Socialism brought nationalism and the traditional German cultural heritage into disrepute. The founding of the Federal Republic of Germany and the German Democratic Republic was meant to prevent a renewed "German catastrophe." The Federal Republic understood itself as legal successor to the Third Reich and perforce the heir of National Socialism (see Lepsius 1989). Nazi guilt was normatively internalized, as M. Rainer Lepsius terms it, and served as a negative basis of legitimacy for the new regime. The German Democratic Republic on the other hand based its identity on the anti-fascist resistance during the Third Reich, externalized the Nazi guilt onto the Federal Republic, was anti-national in its orientation, and sought legitimacy in socialist internationalization. But constituent to both of these successor states was the rejection of all German-national identifications. The collapse of National Socialism as well as those crimes committed by it in the nation's name had discredited German nationalism in both German states.

It is interesting to note how this change was reflected in first names. In the postwar period the percentage of German names declined. That this development was not abrupt but gradual—becoming more precipitous only with the onset of the 1960s—would seem to parallel analyses of political culture in the Federal Republic which show the residual effects of National Socialism on political attitudes (see Conradt 1980).

But the *degree* of the rise and fall of German names varied among population segments. In the previous chapter we saw how secularization processes variously affected Protestants and Catholics, and this was also the case with German names. So let us now place our general findings within this religious context and supplement our Grimma and Gerolstein data with that of Michael Simon, which encompasses three Catholic communities and two Protestant ones. Figure 4.5 shows the percentage of German names in Catholic and Protestant communities from the beginning of the nineteenth century to the end of the twentieth.

Figure 4.5
Percentage of German Names in Catholic and Protestant Communities

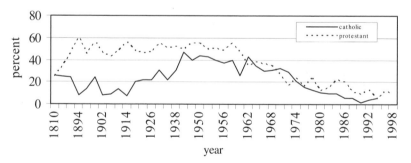

Let us first look at names after the Second World War. Figure 4.5 shows that the turn away from German names began simultaneously and ran a parallel course in the Protestant and Catholic communities. We have already traced this back to the discrediting of nationalism and the traditional German cultural heritage that resulted from defeat in the Second World War and the establishment of the two German states. But the rise in German names began at different points in time in the Protestant and Catholic communities. German names already made up more than 50 percent of all names in Protestant communities at the start of the twentieth century, whereas the percentage of German names in Catholic communities first saw an increase during the First World War and particularly after 1933. The total rise in the percentage of German names from 1914-1945 was almost strictly owing to the increase of German names in Catholic communities.

The trend toward German names in the Protestant communities began much earlier—at the start of the nineteenth century. These divergent patterns require an explanation, and it is to be found in the differing attitudes of Protestants and Catholics to nationalism. As was shown in the last chapter, the ideologies and strategies serving to orient the faithful of both churches also exerted an influence in the area of names. Some historians have interpreted nationalism as a secular religion, and it affected Protestant and Catholic Churches in diametrically opposed fashion.

That Protestants selected German names to a greater degree than Catholics is explicable from the fact that Protestantism had a greater affinity for the idea of nationalism and to the Prussian-led formation of a German nation-state. The close relationship of Protestantism to the state was institutionally prepared and safeguarded with the princely episcopate—the prince combining in his own person the head of state and the highest Protestant bishopric. The various princely episcopates then later merged in the person of the Prussian king (Wallmann 1985: 199), to whom clergymen swore their oath of investiture (Wehler 1995: 1173).

This institutional confluence had its parallel in an ideological harmony of Protestantism and nationalism. The nation-state was viewed as the completion of Protestant Prussia's "German mission" (Wehler 1995: 379). The Protestant Society celebrated German unification with the slogan, "From Luther to Bismarck." The Franco-Prussian War was seen as a *religious* war between Catholics and Protestants. "The Hohenzollern dynasty was regarded as an instrument of divine will in world history, which Protestant Christians were compelled to follow." (Wehler 1995: 383) Thus emerged a national Protestantism, a fusion of Protestant doctrine with the competing religion of nationalism.

This ideological linkage was mirrored in first names to the extent that Protestant parents opted less and less for Christian first names and increasingly for German ones. Michael Simon (1989: 168) demonstrates how the Hohenzollern names of Friedrich and Wilhelm became the most popular names among Protestants at the beginning of the nineteenth century, while Catholics remained unmoved.

The link between nationalism and Protestantism also made the integration of Catholics difficult—they were second-class countrymen (Wehler 1995: 959). Added to this were developments in the Catholic Church itself, which succeeded in consolidating the Catholic milieu in the nineteenth century and in rendering it indifferent to nationalist ideology. After 1803, the Catholic Church developed in two directions. On the one hand the pope succeeded in strengthening the centralist structures of the Church as well as his own authority—Pope Pius IX in particular, whose long tenure (1846-78) enabled him to skillfully fortify and centralize papal power. In 1854, independent of any church council, the dogma of the Immaculate Conception was promulgated, and at the First Vatican Council of 1869-70 the doctrine of papal infallibility was issued (Wallmann 1985: 249). The papacy assumed an increasingly absolutist structure in its attempt to form a heavy bulwark against processes of modernization and secularization. Piety among the Catholic faithful concurrently received a strong new impulse at mid-century (see Sperber 1984), the enormous success of the 1844 Trier pilgrimage to the "Holy Robe" serving as the initial spark.[3] Throughout Germany there was greatly increased participation in village processions and in feast days of patron saints, everywhere Catholic societies were established and religious orders experienced a surge in membership. In the nineteenth century, Catholicism was a vital force that was only strengthened by Bismarck's *Kulturkampf* against the Catholic Church in the 1870s and succeeded in inoculating Catholics against German nationalist sentiment for quite some time. Only toward the end of the long nineteenth century and the outbreak of the First World War were nationalist inroads made among Catholics, who increasingly gave their children German names; between 1933-1945 the percentage was equal to that typical of Protestant communities.

In Gerolstein, in 1913 Kaiser Wilhelm II attended the consecration of the Redeemer Church.[4]

The fact that the Kaiser saw fit to honor the official consecration of the Protestant church had consequences for the christening of children: the name Wilhelm rose in popularity. The cooperative relationship between Protestantism and the state was also depicted in the beautiful mosaic lining the church's dome: on one side are the portraits of Friedrich Barbarossa, Pepin I, Charlemagne, and Kaiser Wilhelm I, while on the other side are those of Martin Luther, Philipp Melanchthon, Boniface, and Willibrord.

Let us sum up. German and Christian names traditionally form the two cultural reference points in the naming of children. At the beginning of the twentieth century over 80 percent of first names were drawn from these two sources. The trajectory of German first names described an upside-down U, steadily increasing from the early nineteenth century to a 50 percent share of all names, leveling out after the Second World War, then sinking to a 5 percent share by the mid-1990s. This cycle varied from Protestant to Catholic communities insofar as the rise in German names among Protestants began in the early-nineteenth century and among Catholics with the outbreak of the First World War.

The rise and fall of German names accompanied the rise and fall of German nationalism. The construction of a nation primarily encompasses the construction of a common history that is linked to names—in our case, German ones. Great founding figures in German history (or so defined) were considered the most desirable namesakes. The upswing in German names was the result of a nationalism that progressed from the beginning of the nineteenth century through German unification and the First World War to its peak in the Nazi years, thus optimizing the chances that children would be given German names. The increase in German names in Protestant communities was likely influenced by the strong affinities Protestantism had for nationalism.

The discrediting of nationalism that came with military defeat and the downfall of National Socialism in 1945 created an environment in which German names were no longer popular. Both successor states abandoned the distinctive hallmarks of nationalism and helped in fact to discredit it. This change of attitude toward the traditional German cultural heritage was reflected in first names, German ones losing in significance and suffering a radical curtailment.

Notes

1. This thesis is not uncontested. John Breuilly (1999) has attempted to show that political nationalism in Germany first became a significant mass phenomenon in the second half of the nineteenth century. However, this does not necessarily contradict our findings insofar as Breuilly is mainly concerned with nationalism as a political strategy.
2. Prussian partisanship and German nationalism cannot of course be equated. With regard to first names, "invention of tradition" would seem to play little role.
3. The Holy Robe was believed to have been worn by Christ. Five hundred thousand people took part in this procession organized by the Bishop of Trier.
4. The photo was taken by J. Becker of Wittlich.

5

Dissolution of Traditional Ties

Family relations can have very different meanings in different societies, ranging from being of very little importance to the organization of social relations to playing a central role in such. Equally various is the importance of blood relations and particularly those between parents and offspring. For the Nayar of Indian Karala, it is not the biological father who raises the children but the mother's brother. The girls have sexual contact with several male partners. If they become pregnant, one of the potential fathers assumes paternity and ends his obligations by paying a sum of money to the mother (cited in Nave-Herz and Onnen-Isemann 2001: 291). That the parent-child relationship in Germany (as well as the family structure in previous centuries) has an entirely different function and value is obvious.

The structure of family relations in general and those between parents and children in particular can be expressed in myriad ways. One of these is through names. Parents can either choose names of family members or relatives in naming their children or they can choose names wholly independent of any familial connection. Naming the child after family members places it in an ancestral continuum that is thereby defined as important. The handing down of family names—or not—is expressive of the importance placed on familial relations. Names frequently express affiliation with the group to the exclusion of others. Claude Levi-Strauss (1968: especially chapter 7) has reconstructed the logic behind classifications of family and family-line relationships through names in simple societies. The Romans had three names, for example, Gaius Julius Caesar, Marcus Tulius Cicero (see Wilson 1998: 4). The first name was the *prenomen* and the personal name of its bearer; the second name was the *nomen* or *gentilicium* and designated the bearer's kinship or lineage; the third name, the *cognomen*, specified either a branch of the family tree or was the name by which a person was called. Personal names in Russia likewise consist of three elements: the first name, the father's name, and the family name, for example, Alexander Sergeevich Pushkin (see Stellmacher 1996: 1726). Names have a very similar structure in Frisian, where family names were introduced only very late. One's family was expressed by passing on the father's name. For example, Antje Gerds would be the daughter of Gerd (Stellmacher 1996: 1727).

We will now analyze the naming of children for family members. Because, as in the last chapter, we are interested in processes of cultural change, we will here examine the changes in familial relations as manifested in the phenomenon of first names. Similar to the secularization thesis in the area of religion, in the sphere of kinship many sociologists have hypothesized that family and relations have suffered a loss in importance and function through modernization processes. Indeed, this thesis is almost as old as the sociological discipline itself. As principal witnesses for this thesis, Friedhelm Neidhart (1975: 67) cites Herbert Spencer and William F. Ogburn. Although assumption of the family's diminishing role is a popular one, the empirical evidence for it is debatable. Sociologists are inclined to see linear trends, and they are being constantly reminded by historians that their hypotheses cannot be historically substantiated. Karl Lenz and Lothar Bönisch (1997) have gone into detail regarding the myths of family sociology. In a survey of historical research findings, Michael Mitterauer (1989) has shown that in different contexts there are different developmental trends with regard to the family, and that one can hardly assert any generalized linear family trends until the early twentieth century. This also holds true for names. In his study *Kinship in Neckarhaus, 1700-1870*, David Sabean demonstrates that the percentage of names carrying on the name of a relative increased rather than decreased over time and that family ties grew stronger rather than weaker. Such findings remind us not to generalize our own findings for a certain time period and to specify their context.

But even for the twentieth century there are studies that show the family did not decrease but rather increased in importance. Bertram (1995) cites research showing that parents support their children longer today than was previously the case. Michael Wagner (1989) has shown that the incidence of children resettling outside of their hometown has decreased rather than increased and that a higher and growing number of children remain in their hometown and in close proximity to their parents. Insofar, there has been no waning of the parent-child relationship through increased mobility. In my opinion, the ambivalent and sometimes contradictory findings are frequently the result of focusing on different dimensions of family relations (see Huinink, Mayer and Wagner 1989). It makes sense to specify (a) the relationships (parent-child, grandparents-grandchildren, nuclear family-extended family) and (b) the content of the relationships (choosing a spouse, nursing the sick, amount of contacts, etc.). This will produce findings that are less contradictory than is seemingly now the case.

Insofar as the names of grandparents and parents are passed down to children—or not—names can be expressive of the parent-child relationship as well as that with other relatives. Naming one's child after its parent or grandparent can be interpreted as an attempt to integrate the child into the family traditions and to simultaneously express the importance of those traditions. It is safe to assume that over time the passing on of kinship ties will recede, and we term this a *decline in the transmission of familial traditions*. This does not mean that the relationships have become less important in other respects.[1] This also does not mean that the frequency and intensity of contacts between parents and children has lessened. According to the findings of Wagner (1989) and Bertram (1995), this is not the case; meaning that family traditions play a less central role in what may be the increased importance of family activities.

Family traditions are transmitted through the handing down of parents' names to their children. When a son is named for his father or a daughter for her mother, we interpret this as a strengthening of family ties and the passing on of family traditions. Research shows that family ties are not maintained solely by naming children after parents. In some instances the father's and mother's names are blended, for instance Gerhard (father) and Gunhild (mother) combine to create Gundhard (son) or Gerhild (daughter) (Seibicke 1996: 1209). Names most frequently passed down are those of the grandparents and blood-relation godmothers and godfathers (Rossi 1965; Simon 1989).

Unfortunately the data of the registry office—in contrast to that of church records—does not include the names of grandparents and godparents, so that we can only use parents' names in testing our thesis of weakening family ties. As such, our measurements are fairly conservative particularly in view of the fact that only one or two children are generally named after the father or mother in a given family because otherwise the children would be indistinguishable from each other. The number of births, however, has receded over time, so that the probability of passing on a name has increased. The fact that only a portion of familial names can be investigated may increase the amount of names that show familial ties, but not the pattern over time—our principal interest.[2]

Figure 5.1
Percentage of Children Named after Parents

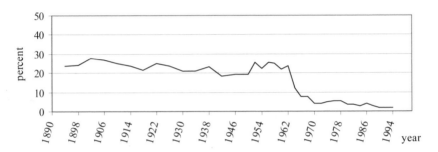

The database for figure 5.1 is Grimma and Gerolstein. For the afore-mentioned reasons, the percentage of children named after their parents is very low. But the results confirm the hypothesis that over time fewer and fewer children were christened with the names of their parents. In 1890, 23.5 percent of children bore parental names, in 1994 it was 3.5 percent. This decrease in the importance of family traditions first manifested itself in the 1950s. Unfortunately in this instance Michael Simon's data cannot help us to place our findings in a wider historical context because he does not list the names of parents and godparents. But if one looks at Simon's graphics (1989: 140, 146, 154) then one sees that naming a child after godparents—who are mainly relatives—and parents suffered a dramatic decrease only toward the end of the nineteenth century. From the seventeenth to the end of the nineteenth century, the percentage of such names remained high. This finding is supported by the results of other studies on the handing down of familial names (see Debus, Hartig, Menke and Schmitz 1973).

How can one explain the lessening importance of family tradi-tions with regard to the handing down of names? In *Wirtschaft und*

Gesellschaft (1980: 212), Max Weber describes the family as an economic provider community. Weber presupposes that the ties between parents and children primarily owe their staying power to the common household. The strict character of household control decreases when the family's importance as an economic provider unit diminishes, thus leading to a divorce between the home and the household enterprise (Weber 1980: 229). Extrapolating from Weber, we can say that the decline in familial names is owing to a decrease in the economic dependence of parents on their children. The less dependence that exists between parents and children, the less is the need and compulsion to give expression to the bond of family traditions.

The economic ties existing between parents and children have been loosened over the years as a result of two factors. With the decrease in the number of people occupied in the agrarian sector, the family has decreased in significance; an individual's subsistence is no longer directly connected to the family but is acquired outside of its framework and has the status of earned income—a family income has been increasingly replaced by individual earned income. This also results in the diminishing importance of family succession and the handing down of tradition (see Mitterauer 1989: 185); at least there is no economic necessity driving it.

The following photo, taken in 1935, shows the integration of several generations of both sexes on a farm.[3]

Over time the percentage of people in the agrarian sector decreased and the extended family as an agricultural production unit became less important. For calculating the percentage of people in the agrarian sector, I have used the data provided by Rüdiger Hohls and Hartmut Kaelble (Hohls and Kaelble 1989). Both authors analyzed job structures in the last hundred years for various regions of Germany, and using this analysis I have calculated the percentage of people in agriculture in Gerolstein (Hohls and Kaelble 1989: 132). There is no such information for Grimma, so we must limit ourselves to Gerolstein. If one considers the percentage of agricultural workers in the total context of jobs, one notes the following development: 1895—62.7 percent, 1907—67 percent, 1925—63.9 percent, 1950—54.7 percent, 1961—38.4 percent, 1970—22.3 percent.[4] By correlating the percentage of agricultural workers with the weakening in family ties through our analysis of names, then one arrives at a correlation coefficient of .84 (Pearson's Correlation).[5] The empirical results thus indicate a strong connection between the number of workers in the primary sector and parents passing on their names to their children.[6]

The greater economic independence of parents from their children has also been the result of social insurance. Its introduction and expansion has relieved the family of having to support older family members or those who have fallen ill or become unemployed (Mayer and Müller 1987). With the introduction of social insurance, the traditional generational contract of a household was made more general and thereby independent of the concrete parent-child relationship. It loosened intra-family bonds, which can often be expressed in the handing down of names from parent to child. One must distinguish among three types of social security: pension funds, unemployment insurance, and health insurance. I have reconstructed the percentage of Germans covered by each type of social security for the period 1894-1970 (see Flora and Alber 1982)[7] and broken it down for specific years.

The development of the social insurance system becomes even more marked when regarding the system as a whole. Below is a figure I have created as an index for the average percentage of people covered by health, pension, and unemployment insurance.

Table 5.1
Percentage of the Socially Insured Population

	1900	1910	1920	1930	1940	1950	1960	1970
Pension fund	21	22	27	31	33	30	37	34
Unemployment Insurance				22	22	20	28	32
Health Insurance	18	22	18	29	29	36	42	43

Figure 5.2
Development of Social Insurance in Germany

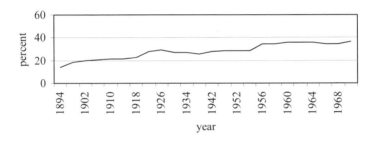

Figure 5.2 and table 5.1 show that there was a continual increase not only in the percentage of people covered by individual insurance plans but by the social security system as a whole. If we correlate the percentage of people covered by a single insurance plan with our figures for the lessening importance of family tradition (again, solely for Gerolstein) then we emerge with a correlation of -.7 for pension insurance, a correlation of -.51 for unemployment insurance, and for health insurance a correlation of -.62. These correlation figures show the expected connection between more extensive coverage by economic insurance and the diminishing importance of the family as measured by the passing down of first names.[8]

The correlation between the percentage of workers in the agrarian sector and the percentage of people covered by insurance on the one hand and the percentage of passed down names on the other is a necessary but insufficient element in tracing a causal connection. I am referring here to the problem of so-called ecological correlation—meaning that although these causal connections may exist at the collective level, they do not have to exist at the individual level. We have already discussed this problem in our introduction with respect to the work of James Coleman, who spoke of the ecological fallacy (1950). Unfortunately there is no data available allowing us to test our findings at the individual level. Our only possibility is to make theoretically plausible why correlations on the aggregate level may also exist on the individual level.

As we have seen, regularities at the collective or macro-level can be explained through the combination of three factors (Coleman 1990, Esser 1996): (1) through the influence of the macro-context on the behavior of individuals (independent variable—society; dependent variable—the individual); (2) as the result of individual actions that determine other actions (independent and dependent variable—individual); and (3) as the consequence of aggregation (independent variable—individual; dependent variable—society). Statistical correlations between aggregate data can be taken as a proof that corresponding relationships exist at the individual level, but only insofar as they can be explained by these three steps. This means that in the case of the relationship between economic protection and the lessening of family influence, we must be able to proceed from the societal level to the individual and from the individual level back to the societal one. In doing so, one emerges with the following argument: (1) The introduction of state economic protection leads to a secure economic existence for the individual and makes him independent of the family's care (link between society and the individual); (2) for those individuals who have economic protection through social insurance, the passing down of family traditions in the form of—among other things—parental first names is less important than it is for the individual who has no economic protection (link between individual and individual level); (3) individuals who do not pass their names on to their children effect a lessening of family influence in the area of names in society at large (link between individual and societal level).

These three assumptions provide the *theoretical* basis for the statistical correlations and help us to explain why family tradition has decreased over the past hundred years. While we have no empirical evidence to illustrate how different forms of economic security and the changing significance of the family are related on the individual level, we can develop a plausible line of argument based on these premises. This is, of course, no empirical proof of a connection at the individual level; however it does show that one can formulate a plausible theoretical argument to support these assumptions.[9]

Our interpretation gains further support through other empirical findings in name research. Louis Bosshart (1973), who investigated first names in the Swiss canton of Schaffhausen, shows that from 1940-1959 every fifth baby boy on average was given the name of his father, and from 1960-1970 every ninth boy. However, farmers as a specific occupational group were much more traditional: 54.4 percent of baby boys from 1940-1944 were named after their fathers or grandfathers. Rudolf Kleinöder (1996) examined a rural area in the Upper Palatinate from the sixteenth century to the present. As source-material he used Protestant parish registers of the imperial count's lands (*Reichsgrafschaft*) of Sulzbürg-Wolfstein and the Catholic parish registers of the neighboring lands of the Bavarian elector (these confessional differences go back to historical factors). Kleinöder comes to the conclusion that fewer and fewer children were named after parents in the course of the twentieth century, and as of 1950 parental names were mainly given to children as second names; even this became less and less frequent starting in the 1970s and 1980s. Achim Masser (1992) comes to a similar conclusion in his study of first names in the South Tyrol. For the timeframe after the Second World War, the author confirms that "the names of parents, godparents, and grandparents played an increasingly smaller role in a period that felt no obligation to uphold earlier traditions. The significantly higher rate [of traditional first names] among boys in comparison to girls shows the stronger integration of male descendants into this tradition, whereas girls were seen as candidates for other, more modern names." (Masser 1992: 56). Dieter Stellmacher (1996: 1726) summarizes the research findings and concludes: "Both heirs of the farm and those inheriting the (bourgeois) family business were as a rule very consciously named after a male ancestor, mostly the father or grandfather."

Let us draw up a balance sheet. The structure of family relations can find its expression in a variety of hallmarks, among these first names. Parents can choose names from among their relatives or immediate family, or they can avail themselves of completely other names. The handing down of names from grandparents and parents can be interpreted as the attempt to integrate the newborn into the family tradition and by so doing assert the importance of that tradition. We have been operating under the assumption that over time the passing down of traditional family ties decreases, and this our analysis has shown. It appears to have become less important for parents to place their offspring in a traditional family continuum, they resort ever more frequently to names not their own. This implies a more open structure in which other factors can exercise influence, factors which we will shortly be analyzing in closer detail. The family's decreasing importance in the sphere of names is owing to the increased economic independence of parents from children and vice-versa. Traditional family ties have become less necessary with the advent of earned income outside the household as opposed to cooperative work on the farm, and with the replacement of family solidarity through a comprehensive social insurance system.

Notes

1. Martin Diewald (1991) has shown that distinguishing between various dimensions in relationships can be of real empirical significance. For the individual, the family in its support capacity takes on various degrees of importance. Whereas friendships provide a more positive relationship in the sense of socializing and sharing hobbies or interests, family and relations are clearly more important for their psychic and time investments, for example in caring for the sick. This function of the family has not changed over the years, while friendship relations have increased in importance.
2. This is based on the assumption that the relation of parents/grandparents names has remained constant.
3. The photo is courtesy of Heinrich Rochus.
4. Although unavailable for Grimma, there exists comparative data for East Germany as a whole. This data shows that there was a similar development among workers in the agricultural and forestry sectors: 1950—28 percent, 1955—22 percent, 1960—17 percent, 1965—15 percent, 1970—13 percent, 1975—11 percent, 1980—11 percent (see Rytlewski and Opp de Hipt 1987: 66).
5. In calculating this correlation, the percentage of agricultural workers was interpolated in a linear fashion. If instead of the linear interpolated figures, however, one uses the original data from six different points in time, then there is a correlation of .81.
6. In correlating time-lines, pseudo-correlations can sometimes emerge as the result of auto-correlation structures common to both variables. Therefore, I have done a time-line analysis and factored in a Cochrane-Orcutt model (Pinkyck and Rubinfield 1991). The coefficient of this model, a standardized B-value, is .83 (significance level: 0.1 percent).
7. Such a reconstruction was impossible for Gerolstein and Grimma, as there was no available data.
8. Our calculation is once more based on the Cochrane-Orcutt model. The coefficients are -.73, -.69 and -.62 (on a significance level of 1 or 5 percent).

9.　　I make three contentions regarding the decrease in agricultural workers:

1)　　The decrease leads to people earning their economic livelihood in an area no longer connected with agricultural work, thus being no longer reliant on the family for sustenance.

2)　　For individuals who are no longer economically reliant on the family, the family mediation of tradition—on the basis of, among other things, the naming of children after parents—becomes decreasingly important.

3)　　The existence of individuals for whom the mediation of tradition on the basis of passing down first names has become less important, leads to the lessening importance of the family in terms of names in society at large.

6

Rise of the Individual

In our analysis of names we have regarded society as a unit, without entering into an examination of possible sub-groups and their characteristics. Since the earliest beginnings of sociology, sociologists have described sub-groups and social structures in terms of social inequality. All persons belonging to a certain class have equal access to certain resources (income, education, power, and prestige) in constructing their lives. At the same time, each class demarcates itself from other strata that have lesser or greater access to these resources. The result is a social structure consisting of layered strata. In the following pages we will pursue the question as to whether the various social strata are likewise various in their choice of first names (see Debus 1968; 1996; Shin 1980). We will begin our inquiry by testing Ulrich Beck's individuation theory, which is premised on the decreasing importance of social strata in determining behavior. We will investigate whether in the course of the twentieth century there has in fact been a process of individuation and, if so, how it might be explained (first subsection); we will then examine whether stratum-specific names have decreased over time (second subsection); finally we will describe in greater detail the ways in which these strata try to distinguish themselves from one another (third subsection).

Social-Structural Change and Individuation

It is very seldom that sociological descriptions of a society's structure are absorbed into the consciousness of the broader public. Ulrich Beck's "individuation thesis" has transcended its academic origins to enjoy popular acceptance. With the publication of his *Risk Society* (1986), Beck's thesis has become a commonplace of present-day sociology and it has triggered a plethora of discussions, critiques, and revisions (see Ebers 1995, Beck and Sopp 1997, Friedrichs 1998, Kippele 1998, Kron 2000, Schnell and Kohler 1995, Müller 1997, Huinink and Wagner 1998, Burkhart 1998, Junge 2002). But the individuation concept—despite or because of the boom in scholarly and public discussion of individuation processes—has remained unfocused and polyvalent. We cannot here recapitulate the many definitions, criticisms and diagnoses. Let us rather focus the discussion with two questions: How do individuation processes impinge on first names? Can one ascertain individuation processes at work across time, and if so then how can these be explained?

I would like to make two conceptual qualifications right here at the start. First, individuation is a term that indicates social change. Monika Wohlraub-Sahr (1997) denotes two levels at which social change can take place with regard to individuation. On a social-structural level changes in the division of labor, in social differentiation and class affiliations can lead to individuation. One can also denote a discursive level separate from the social-structural one. This discursive level is the public, cultural definition as to whether an individual himself or the collective he belongs to is responsible for his actions. Hence, individuality means a culturally defined sense of individual responsibility. In the following we will limit our inquiry to the social-structural changes leading to the rise of individuality in the sense of distinctive personalities. Secondly, Gertrud Nunner-Winkler (1985) differentiates between an inner and outward individuality. A person can be perceived and described as an individual, and they can also perceive themselves that way. We are limiting our analysis to the external perception of individuality: parents bestow a certain name on a child and thereby give it an external label. We assume that the type of name will show whether it is important to parents to express the individuality of their child and to set it apart from others.

Following Ulrich Beck (1995), one can distinguish two phases and two notions of the individuation process. The first notion was elaborated by two classic sociologists, Emile Durkheim and Georg Simmel. Both describe the developmental path toward modern society as a process of increasing differentiation and division of labor. For Simmel (1983: 305ff.) the effects of the differentiation processes for the formation of individuality are to be found in his concept of the intersection of social circles. Individuality first emerges when a person's field of action is so heterogeneous that he himself forms a point of intersection for various circles in a highly specific way, dissimilar to any other person. The more varied people's life conditions are, the more individual will be their tastes. This same theory is the basis of Durkheim's theory of the division of labor: "The individual personality develops first with the division of labor." (1977: 444) What Durkheim mostly means by division of labor is the teasing out of specific skills that distinguish—that is, individuate—one person from the next in their chosen area of work.[1]

This notion of the connection between differentiating processes and the formation of individuality is also at the root of the concept of role differentiation and role-identities. The role structure of a functionally differentiated society demands that the individual anticipate and meet widely varying role expectations. He/she is a fiscal officer and member of a basketball team as well as a single mother/father, etc. The multiplicity of role expectations makes it probable that only a few other persons will embody a similar combination of roles, so that the respective cluster of role expectations attains a singular status (Schimank 2000).

Individuation is a concept for designating a process of modernization in which people share fewer common characteristics and are thereby increasingly distinguishable from one another. Such an understanding of individuation links up with the etymological meaning of the term.[2] "In-dividuum" is the Latin root and means "the indivisible"; in this sense one can attribute more individuality to someone the less features he has in common with others. The distinctiveness can express itself in manifold ways. The following photos show two school classes. The first photo is from Gerolstein in the 1920s,[3] and the second one is my son's class from the year 2000.

The expression of individuality through clothes, haircut, and posture is much more evident in the second photo and points to a marked individuation trend over time. Our definition of individuation processes plugs in very nicely to first names. The fewer people who bear the same name, the more people there are who can be seen as distinctive entities, and greater individuation thus exists. Accordingly, we have sought to determine how many different names, that is, unique names there were per year; by unique we mean a name given to no other child in the year of our sample (Lieberson and Mikelson 1995: 930). And we have placed the number of unique

names in relation to the total number of names per year (each comprising 100) and have defined these quotients as an individuation index. We are operating here under the assumption that the individuation index has risen over time. Figure 6.1 shows the results. The database is Grimma and Gerolstein.

Over the course of the twentieth century there was indeed a change toward increasing individuation.[4] While in 1894, 38 percent of the names given were unique, one hundred years later 81 percent of names were. The process of individuation was almost complete by the beginning of the 1950s; thereafter the individuation index increased only very slightly.[5]

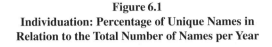

Figure 6.1
Individuation: Percentage of Unique Names in
Relation to the Total Number of Names per Year

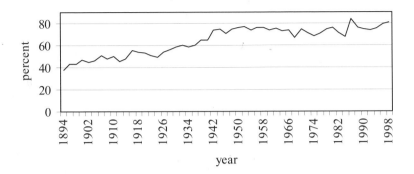

The developmental trend of increasing individuation can be seen in the following examples. In Gerolstein in 1894, 70 percent of all male newborns bore the five most popular male names (Johann, Mathias, Peter, Joseph, Nicolaus). In 1994 only 28 percent of male newborns bore the five most popular male names (Daniel, David, Lukas, René, Andreas). Female names follow a similar pattern. In 1894, 63 percent of baby girls bore the five most popular girls' names (Katharina, Anna, Maria, Magdalena, Elisabeth), whereas in 1994 it was 26 percent of the five most popular names (Katharina, Laura, Sarah, Julia, Michelle). It appears that over time parents felt it increasingly important to distinguish their children—to individuate them—from others by giving them less popular names.

Before we speak of the origins of this process of increasing individuation, I should like to address three aspects of this finding.

1. The individuation index's point of reference is the relationship between the number of unique names and the total number of names *per time point*. The individuation index achieves the same result for two consecutive age groups, even if the same names are used for both age groups. However, if one imagines two children one year apart but with the same name meeting each other in kindergarten or in grade school, it becomes clear that our measurement of individuation can be problematic due to the fact that diversity of names cannot be guaranteed. Therefore, in addition to the individuation index, we have calculated the number of newly introduced names per statistical period. Parents introducing new names distinguish their children not only from those in their same age group but from those in

the previous age-group. But the second measurement of individuation processes comes to a very similar result: the percentage of newly introduced names climbed steadily from the end of the nineteenth century to the mid-twentieth.

2. With the help of Michael Simon's data we have attempted to place our findings along a broader historical continuum and examine whether the individuation process of the twentieth century issued from an even earlier individuation process. The result of this examination (whose results we cannot detail here) shows that individuation was in fact a phenomenon that first gained purchase in the twentieth century, for the individuation index is consistently low from the seventeenth century to the end of the nineteenth.

3. Finally, we have examined whether Protestants and Catholics differed from one another in their degree of individuation. A priori, this is to be expected. In his study of suicide (1983), Durkheim linked up the process of individuation with religion. Durkheim called Protestantism the first individual religion because the individual believer was to a large extent the creator of his own faith through a personal interpretation of the Bible, the elimination of any authoritative mediation between the believer and God, and the relatively small degree of normative regulation of everyday life. Thou shalt be an individual was the new commandment: "Today no one any longer contests the binding nature of the rule that orders us to be a person and to strive for ever greater personhood." (Durkheim 1977: 445). If one compares the individuation index in Catholic Gerolstein with Protestant Grimma, one sees in fact that the latter's degree of individuation was consistently 10 percent more than the former. Michael Simon's data reflects a similar pattern.

Classic thinkers of sociology have traced the beginnings of the individuation process to an increasing division of labor. A multitude of activities and roles makes the individual into someone unique. It is no easy task to empirically measure the process of role differentiation. I have limited myself to an examination of the degree of occupational differentiation because there exists empirical data covering a longer time frame. Using the data of Rüdiger Hohls and Hartmut Kaelble (1989) I have come up with a heterogeneity index for the occupational structure of the Gerolstein region.[6] The heterogeneity index is high, if the employed persons are distributed equally across the number of occupational groups. By the same token, if gainfully employed persons tend to concentrate in just a few occupational groups, this constitutes a low heterogeneity index. The calculated index of occupational heterogeneity rose from 59 in 1895 to 89 in 1970, thus signifying an increase in occupational heterogeneity. If we correlate this measurement of occupational heterogeneity with our measurement of individuation, we emerge with a correlation of .86.[7] Thus there is a statistical link between occupational differentiation and individuation.[8] One cannot statistically prove that this correlative link is a causal one because as in preceding chapters we are dealing here with the problem of ecological fallacy. The supposition of causality in this case is merely a theoretical supposition of plausibility.

Dissolution of Class Ties

Ulrich Beck and Elisabeth Beck-Gensheim place the end of the second phase of individuation—the actual focus of their analysis—at about the mid-twentieth century. They connect individuation processes with the destructuring of social strata and classes and the dissolution of social milieus. Ulrich Beck (Beck 1983, 1995; Beck and Beck-Gernsheim 1995) denotes two phases of modernization toward the individuated society. According to his thesis, in the first phase a stratified society that is closely linked with a religious-transcendent ideology is replaced by a modern industrial society. The dissolution of traditional ties is compensated for by the emergence of new, class-specific ligatures. Each person is not only member of a certain class or stratum with access to certain resources, but simultaneously belongs to a social milieu linked with this class/stratum. For their part, these class-specific milieus to a large degree structure the lifestyles of their members, defining family roles and the requirements for membership in milieu-specific associations as well as influencing the way one votes and spends one's free time.

The second phase of modernization, according to Beck, is distinguished by class-specific milieus losing in importance and eventually disappearing, with the resultant emergence of a society beyond class and strata. When class-specific ties are dissolved, then individuals are freed from the last bastion of collective meaning; they themselves must create meaning in their lives (Hitzler and Honer 1995). The dissolution of the interpretive power of class-specific milieus is of a piece with changes in the family. Pre-assigned male and female roles as well as those of parents and children lose their normative power. The family structure becomes a sphere for negotiating differences that can only be stabilized over time. For the individual this means that he can no longer rely upon normatively stabilized certainties, that he as an individual must now hash out differences with other individuals and establish rules of coexistence. In such a way does individuation become a normative requirement; humans are damned to individuation (in relation to Sartre, see Beck and Beck-Gernsheim 1993: 179). This idea of individuation accords nicely with our schema. The newborn does not choose his name himself—he receives it from his parents. If this name is no longer based on the traditions of religion, kinship or social stratum but rather serves to distinguish the child from other children, then from the child's perspective one can indeed speak of the damnation to individuality.

The thesis of the diminishing importance of classes and social strata is hotly debated. But as in prior chapters, it is worthwhile specifying in exactly what areas and ways the postulated dissolution takes place. The "hardware" of a class and stratum structure is defined through people's unequal access to resources. The class concept strongly accents the rootedness of social groups in the production sphere of the economy as well as elucidating their clashing differences; whereas the stratum concept concentrates on the distribution of important resources such as income, prestige and education, while deemphasizing any conflicts between strata. Because we are here concerned with the distribution of resources, the stratum concept is the more suitable one.

Dissolution of the strata structure would mean that unequal access to these resources has lessened over time. Karl Ulrich Mayer (1989: 303) summarized various empirical studies and came to the conclusion that intergenerational mobility had not increased over time; this means that a decline in social stratification in the sense of transmitting the inherited stratum to the new generation had not taken place. Rainer Geissler comes to a similar conclusion (1996). Geissler tests the thesis of a dissolution of class and stratum by determining the percentage of various strata in schools and universities. He shows that while the percentage of all strata at institutes of higher learning has increased, the *relative* differences between strata have remained—in fact, to some degree have increased. According to Geissler, this stability in social stratification applies not only to education but also to incomes. He concludes that the social structure has not essentially changed and that one cannot speak of a destratification of German society.

Beck easily parries criticism of his thesis of the dissolution of classes and strata by asserting that his notion of destratification does not concern the access to hard resources. Indeed, one can even speak of destratification when such inequalities have become more acute. For one can distinguish between the access to resources and the "software" of lifestyles. If one sees stratification (defined by unequal access to resources) as independent variables and habits and lifestyle as dependent ones, then one may assume that the link between strata and specific lifestyles has become weaker over time. Granted the relative constancy of unequal access to resources, the destratification thesis would then mean that the connection between resource-conditioned stratification and certain lifestyles has become more tenuous (Geissler 1996: 333). But if classes and strata have become less distinguishable in their public lifestyles, then one would assume that the "hardware" of class and stratum has broken down; but it has only gone from being visible to being latent.

Ulrich Beck (1986) sees the most important reason for this change in the so-called elevator effect, namely the dramatic increase in life expectancy, leisure time, and material prosperity for the entire West German population.[9] The social significance of inequality is thus tempered by this rise in prosperity and the increased security afforded by the welfare state. But the presumed breakdown in class- and stratum-specific lifestyles was followed by a restructuring through new forms of community based on homogenous social milieus. This is less Ulrich Beck's idea than that of Gerhard Schulze as formulated in his *Erlebnisgesellschaft* (1992), a study of modern lifestyles. People with similar lifestyles are part of a postmodern society in which the milieu to which they belong has been partly created by the leisure industry. The argument is as follows: (1) Increased prosperity and welfare (elevator effect) leads to more leisure time, and more leisure time allows one to style one's own life; (2) class and stratum thereby play a diminished role in determining one's lifestyle; (3) thus leading to either a plurality of individual lifestyles (Beck) or to new forms of community based on similar lifestyles within certain social milieus (Schulze).

I have addressed the destratification thesis so as to situate the results of our own analysis of stratum-specific names within the scholarly discussion and to specify their relevance. I see first names as an aspect of one's lifestyle. To what extent has the influence of stratum on first names diminished over the years? I also see first names as an expression of parental taste. It was Georg Simmel who first stated the idea—later refined by Pierre Bourdieu (1982) and Gerhard Schulze (1992)—that taste in practice was nothing innate but rather served purposes of stratification. Thus, first names are an expression of personal taste that simultaneously functions as a social delineator. Parents use first names to denote (for themselves and others) the stratum to which they and their child feel akin. Thus the name of a world-famous pop star or soccer player is the expression of a popular taste typical of the lower strata and will likely be avoided by those in the educated middle class, who may tend toward names from Greek mythology, thus marking them as educated. If one can assume that names will generally differ from stratum to stratum, destratification in the area of names would mean that these differences decrease over time. Mind you, such a destratification would not concern access to the resources of education and income but is to be understood as the destratification of lifestyles.

We assume that first names as indicators of a stratum's lifestyle are conditioned by access to cultural capital (Bourdieu 1982). One's taste is refined through cultural capital acquired via parents or school. Unfortunately we can measure cultural capital only very roughly. Registry office data indicate parental occupations, and I have divided these into three groups: low qualified, qualified, and highly qualified occupations. Classical class theory would expect that the three different strata would make use of different names. A destratification over time would mean that the fund of common names among strata increases to the extent that the strata are no longer distinguishable. In testing this thesis, I proceeded in the following manner. I measured the educational level of parents based on the father's occupation (classified as "low qualified," "qualified," and "highly qualified"); in order to have a sufficient number for each educational-level stratum, we aggregated the different time points into seven periods. Then I totaled the names common to all three strata in each period. The total number of differing names per period served as the percentage basis. Thus 40 percent would mean that in a given period 40 percent of all names were shared by all three strata. Figure 6.2 shows the results.

As figure 6.2 shows, there are absolutely no indications of a destratification in the area of names. Rather the opposite. Shared names at all levels of society have decreased over time. Names shared among the three educational levels made up 46 percent of all names

Figure 6.2
Percentage of Shared Names by Three Different Classes

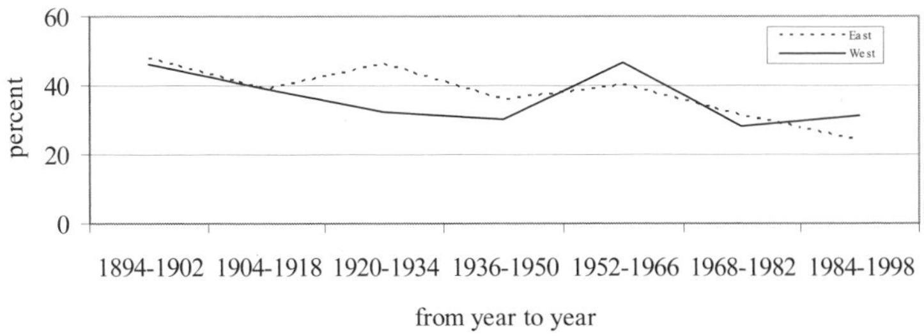

from year to year

at the beginning of the twentieth century, whereas by the end of the century they comprised only 28 percent; that is, the percentage of stratum-specific names increased. Beck hypothesizes that the second half of the twentieth century was a period of destratification, but the facts of the case are just the opposite. Interestingly, this finding holds true not only for the West German town of Gerolstein but also for the East German (1949-1990) town of Grimma. There are no recognizable indicators of progress toward a classless society as envisaged by the GDR leadership and as a growing homogenization of names would necessarily show. The strata differences have not decreased but rather increased.[10]

We can now draw up a balance sheet. In the last one hundred years there has been a potent rise in individuality to the extent that the heterogeneity of names for the child population has increased. Over time parents have attempted to secure the individuality of their children through names. Classic sociology would explain this development through the increasing intersection of social circles. And, in fact, there is a statistical link between the heterogeneity of first names and the heterogeneity of the occupational structure.

Interestingly enough, however, the process of individuation was already complete by the 1950s. With regard to names, the second wave of individuation as presupposed by Ulrich Beck and Elisabeth Beck-Gernsheim never took place. This finding is supported by the lack of destratification in the area of first names: the differences among the various strata did not disappear, in fact names become increasingly stratum-specific. The destratification and individuation hypotheses with regard to the second phase of individuation are two sides of the same coin. The empirical results of our investigation confirm neither the one nor the other hypothesis.

But it would be going too far in saying that our little heuristic of "first names" is a sufficient proof of the validity or non-validity of Beck's destratification and individuation hypotheses. But staying within the realm of first names, we can indeed assert that no destratification process has taken place and that the individuation process was not in the period supposed by Beck—in addition to having other causes than the dissolution of classes and strata.

First Names as Cultural Capital

The stratification theory assumes that people will try to defend or increase their access to resources so as to maintain or improve their relative position in the social structure. If one interprets the naming of a child as an attempt to maintain or improve one's relative position in the social stratum, then one has to take into account that names are a very specific "resource." There is free and equal access to all legal names including those employed by elites along with their affiliations of prestige. Not only is there unrestricted access to a society's pool of names, in contrast to other matters of taste the naming of a child is not dependent on access to material resources (see Besnard 1994: 166; and especially Lieberson 2000). Stanley Lieberson makes the argument, that whereas a flight to the premiere of an opera at La Scala or dining at a five-star restaurant or a fancy holiday in Greece or the purchase of fashionable clothes are all predicated not only on a certain cultural capital but on considerable financial outlay, such resources are irrelevant to the choice of a child's first name. The fact that all first names are open to all individuals regardless of their resources allows people from the lower strata to gain status by appropriating the names of the higher strata. The exclusion of the lower strata by the upper strata in matters of taste is always a temporary one. Distinction can be reestablished vis-à-vis the lower strata only if new names are introduced or old ones reinvented. This basic constellation would thus lead us to expect that (1) the upper strata exhibit anti-cyclical behavior with respect to names, avoiding popular names and preferring less popular ones, and that (2) over time there is a diffusion process in which names are first introduced by the upper strata and then trickle downward. Let us examine these hypotheses.

1. We have divided strata into three groups according to the father's level of qualification and have examined to what extent each of the three groups uses the twenty most frequent names. Among parents

in the low-qualified group, 22.6 percent availed themselves of the twenty most frequent names; this was the case with 16.6 percent of parents from the medium-qualified group; and with 16.1 percent of parents from the highly qualified group. This basically confirms our theoretical expectation that parents with low qualifications are more likely to choose fashionable names than the other two groups. But the difference here is negligible.[11]

The differences become much greater when we use a cultural classification of names. We have already seen how Christian and German cultural traditions were the two upon which parents typically drew for names and that both of these traditions lost their importance over time. But this applied to our three categories of strata in varying degrees, as the following two figures show.

Figure 6.3
Class-Specific Use of Christian Names During
Two Different Periods

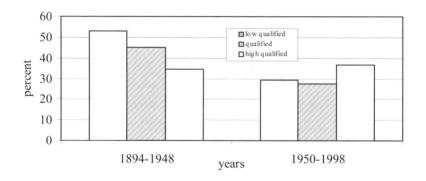

In the first period (1894-1948), in which Christian names predominated, highly qualified households were clearly behind the other two strata in choosing these type names. By the second phase (1950-1998), things had changed completely. Just as Christian names were suffering a big dip in popularity, highly qualified households were now choosing Christian names more often than they had in the first period. This is also the case (if in a less pronounced fashion) regarding transnational names, that is, those from other cultures.

In the next chapter we will see that transnational names grew popular after the Second World War. Granted that highly qualified households were opting for these names more frequently than they had in

Figure 6.4
Class-Specific Use of Transnational Names During Two Different Periods

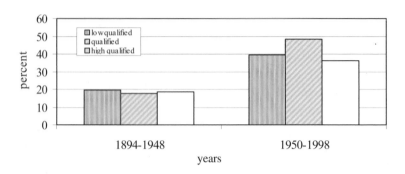

the past, in comparison to the other two strata they remained slightly more reticent.

2. Let us now test our second hypothesis that new first names are introduced by the higher strata and over time trickle down to other strata.[12] My measurement of diffusion processes among the three strata I used is borrowed from Stanley Lieberson and Eleanor O. Bell (1992). I have chosen two time periods separated by a generation—1966-72 and 1990-94. Names not in the top twenty in 1966-72 that entered the top twenty in 1990-94 are those that were diffused to a wider public. So we are focusing on what percentage of these names were used by the three respective strata between 1966-72 and 1990-94. If our diffusion hypothesis is correct, then the new names should have been first introduced by the upper stratum and then increasingly adopted by other strata. Figure 6.4 shows the diffusion of first names.[13]

The empirical findings meet our expectations on several counts. New names were first introduced by highly qualified households. Persons with qualified occupations followed the lead of the highly qualified and adopted this new mode of distinction and became the real protagonists of new names by employing them to an even greater extent than the highly qualified. Low-qualified households also adopted the new names albeit at a slower rate. But the findings only partly correspond to our theoretical expectations. For one, the differences among the three strata in the choice of newly introduced names are slight. For another, the low qualified increasingly adopted the newly introduced names, but always to a lesser degree than the

Figure 6.5
Diffusion of Popular Names Among Class (1966-72 to 1990-94)

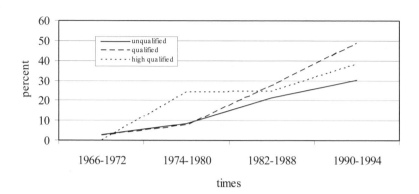

highly qualified. Theoretically speaking, one might have expected that the low qualified would have surpassed the highly qualified in choosing newly introduced names at least by the end of our time frame.

One discovers equally mixed findings in other studies dealing with the diffusion of first names. Rex Taylor (1974) studied the birth registers of Richmond, Virginia in the years 1913, 1930, 1950, and 1968 to ascertain whether the supplementary name "junior" was employed equally across society. He concluded that "junior" started out being used more frequently in the white-collar milieu but that over time it was picked up by blue-collar occupations while concomitantly waning in white-collar ones until by 1968 its usage in both groups was pretty much equal. Stephen Wilson (1998: 331) reports a study done comparing the first names of birth announcements in the London *Times* with those of the general populace. The *Times* is the newspaper of choice of Britain's educated class, and the study showed that names frequently mentioned in the paper's birth notices were taken up a few years later by the general populace. Wilson concludes therefrom that the educated classes served as trendsetters. Philippe Besnard and Guy Desplanques (1986) have shown that between 1890 and 1985 first names trickled down the social pyramid. Stanley Lieberson (2000: 147), in his study of names in Texas between 1965 and 1990, has another finding: "35 percent of the names fit the theory in which higher strata are the first to drop commonly shared tastes, but the remaining 65 percent of names are either given up by both groups at the same time or are abandoned even earlier by mothers of low SES "[14] (Lieberson 2000: 149). Lieberson also criticizes other studies on the stratum-specific diffusion of names because of their imprecision and attempts an explanation of why theory generally fails to prove out. In his study of names in Jena, Stefan Hornbostel (1997: 411) comes to a conclusion similar to our own: "A hierarchical diffusion process is not to be discerned, even granting that top names survive longer in the less-educated group than in the educated stratum from which they originate."

Philippe Besnard and Cyril Grange (1993) have forwarded a possible explanation for these bare differences among strata. They believe that strata distinctions in the past were predicated on time-staggered access to the pool of first names, thereby ushering in a diffusion process. Insofar as recent history goes, Besnard and Grange assert that strata distinctions have evinced themselves in *different* names. This seems to me plausible, particularly in view of the fact that after 1949 the percentage of total names and that of transnational names (see chapter 7) considerably increased, thus increasing the pool of names that might serve to demarcate one stratum from another. It remains for future studies to ascertain whether this is in fact correct.

Notes

1. Markus Schroer (1990) classifies Durkheim as well as Simmel as theorists of "positive individuation."
2. Apart from the terminological fuzziness, another lack in the discourse concerning individuation processes—although we are dealing here with a descriptive category of social change—seems to be mid-term and long-term empirical analyses supporting or refuting the theory (Burkhart 1993: 173).
3. The photo is courtesy of Franz Josef Ferber.
4. One must however take into consideration that the names in the registry office records could have been different from the names children were called by. It is impossible to ascertain whether the effective degree of individuation was not in essence higher as a result of the names children were known by.
5. Stefan Hornbostel (1997) arrives at a very similar result in his study of names in Jena.
6. The heterogeneity index was calculated according to the equation $H = 100 \, (1 - \text{sum total } p^2)$, in which H is the heterogeneity index and p the percentage of individual occupational groups relative to the sum total of gainfully employed. The following are indices for sample years: 1895—59; 1907—54; 1935—58; 1950—68; 1961—81; 1970—89. In calculating the heterogeneity index I have used the Herfindahl-Hirschman index of industrial concentration. For a discussion of this index, see Taagepera and Lee Ray (1977).

7.   This correlation rests on a linear interpolation of the results of the heterogeneity index for the period under investigation. If instead of the linear interpolated results one uses the original results of the six measured time frames, we emerge with a correlation of .82.

8.   Additionally I have conducted a time-series analysis and used a Cochrane-Orcutt model. The co-efficient has a value of .65 and is significant at 1 percent level.

9.   This diagnosis is empirically verifiable. Between 1949 and 1973 real wages in West Germany "increased fourfold and were thereby far above relatively modest increases in real income and real wages during those prosperous phases of the long nineteenth century" (Ambrosius and Kaelble 1992: 17).

10.   While in the other chapters we were able to place our empirical findings within a long-term historical context by testing them against Michael Simon's data, we are unable to confirm a destratification process for the centuries preceding because Simon does not designate parental occupations.

11.   In his study of names in Heidelberg between 1961 and 1976, Kwang Sook Shin (1980) was more definite. He concluded that in comparison to lower social strata the upper middle class tended to draw far more frequently from the pool of less popular names.

12.   Volker Kohlheim (1988) has analyzed the diffusion of first names in the Middle Ages in a study of Regensburg.

13.   I have also analyzed the periods 1942-46 to 1966-72. My hypothesis could not be tested against earlier time periods because the number of cases in the highly qualified category was too small. Nevertheless, one comes to much the same result in grouping the highly qualified with the qualified.

14.   "SES" is Lieberson's abbreviation for socioeconomic status.

7

Globalization

Chapters 3 and 4 showed that the German and Christian cultural traditions decreased in importance over time and additionally that the practice of bestowing the parent's name upon the child has gradually disappeared. Our analysis has also shown that the number of names per year has increased and thus the probability that a newborn will have a different name from other children of his cohort. We have described this as a process of individuation. When one considers these developments as a whole one can then see that first names increasingly freed themselves from a number of constraints and became instruments for expressing greater individuality. This loosening of traditional ties took place mainly after the Second World War.[1]

In this chapter we will analyze whether previously foreign names gained in popularity following the loosening of traditional ties and whether processes of globalization and transnationalization have played a role.

Globalization between Americanization and Creolization

The globalization of daily life is often causally linked with the structures and strategies of global business. According to this thesis, "global players," with their headquarters chiefly in America, produce goods and distribute these through a worldwide network of branch offices and create demand for them through advertising and marketing that in most cases affiliates the product with a Western or American lifestyle. The result is a worldwide homogenization of consumer habits and lifestyles. The global reach of brands such as Nike, Coca-Cola, and McDonalds is frequently cited as an example of the industrially manufactured globalization of everyday life.

This basic theory of a worldwide standardization of daily life was first formulated in 1947 by Theodor W. Adorno and Max Horkeimer in *Dialektik der Aufklärung* (*The Dialectic of Enlightenment*) in the chapter "Kulturindustrie: Aufklärung als Massenbetrug" ("The Culture Industry: Enlightenment as Mass Deception"). Without altering its basic idea, this theory has since been modified and expanded (Hoskins and Mirus 1988; Schiller 1989; Thompson 1995; Thomsen 1995). Benjamin Barber (1996) describes the process as "McWorld." George Ritzer (1995) speaks of a McDonaldization of culture.

The authors tending to doubt the notion of the Americanization of daily life through consumer goods are primarily those who examine the acting subject from a micro-sociological perspective. All "interpretative" sociological approaches are premised on the notion that humans act on the basis of meanings that they derive from the world's objects (see Blumer 1962). The same holds true for the acquisition of consumer items. It is an empirically open question whether and to what degree certain lifestyles connected with consumer goods are adopted, adapted, or rejected. Ulf Hannerz asserts that the acquisition of goods distributed worldwide is done based on their respective cultural relevance. Thus, there is a local adaptation of globally distributed goods, the resultant interaction leading to "creolization." Jan Nederveen Pieterse (1998) makes a similar argument. Cultural influence is not a one-way street that breeds uniformity. In order to describe the peculiar mix of goods on the one hand and their adaptation on the other, the author proposes the term "hybridization." And Roland Robertson (1998) cautions against equating globalization of culture with its homogenization. Instead, according to Robertson, we are experiencing a penetration of global goods and their local adaptation that can be termed "glocalization."

Both the creolization and cultural imperialism theories have their theoretical and empirically weak aspects. Creolization, hybridization, and glocalization are very catchy terms that lend themselves to rich metaphor, but it is unclear what precisely they are supposed to mean and how these theoretical constructs can be made empirically operational so as to undertake scientific measurements. The same criticisms goes for the cultural imperialism theory. Its advocates frequently remain at the abstract level, able only to cite certain illustrative examples without solidly substantiating their theory. There is no distinction drawn between the conditions which exist in country X as opposed to country Y that might shed some light on various degrees of Americanization in different countries.

Through an examination of first names over the past one hundred years I will show that one can work with both theories of the globalization of daily life, but that one must specify their theoretical content and their explanatory relevance. First, I will look at the extent to which a transnationalization of first names has taken place; then I will attempt to locate the reasons for this; and finally I will analyze why certain (formerly) foreign names should have enjoyed such success in Germany and why other names have not been as successful.

Transnationalization Instead of Globalization

We have replaced the term globalization with that of transnationalization (de Swaan 1995), and other authors speak of the denationalization of society (Zürn 1998; Beisheim et al. 1999). I find transnationalization preferable to globalization (see Gerhards and Rössel 1999) because (1) the term defines a starting point of developmental processes within nation-state societies; (2) the term keeps open whether the development is one of globalization, Europeanization, or Americanization; and (3) in the early work of Karl Deutsch (1956) the term is defined as a relational concept that sets the interactions or transactions within a social unit in relation to interactions and transactions with entities lying outside that social unit; this has the advantage of taking into account the fact that along with transnational communication there can simultaneously be increased internal communication that remains unexpressed in any absolute measure of transnationalization processes.

It is in this sense of transnationalization that I have attempted to chart how the relationship between Christian and German names on the one hand and "foreign" names on the other have changed over time.

Figure 7.1 shows that over time there was indeed an increase in names of non-Christian and non-German cultural origin. Whereas in 1894 only 25 percent of names came from foreign cultures, by the end of the twentieth century more than 65 percent did. This increase in transcultural names began in the 1950s. Albeit at a slightly higher level, this process was as marked in Protestant Grimma (part of East Germany from 1949 to 1990) as it was in Catholic Gerolstein (part of West Germany from 1949 to 1990) (see Naumann, Schlimpert, and Schultheis 1986). Both towns witnessed a dramatic receptivity toward previously alien cultures.

Figure 7.1
Transnationalization of First Names (Percentage of Non-Christian and Non-German Names)

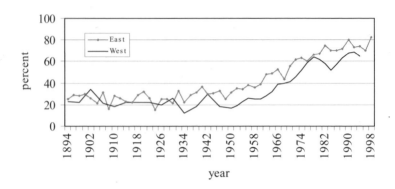

I have used Michael Simon's data to check whether this transnationalization process has a history going back further than the 1950s, and the answer is no. The percentage of non-German and non-Christian names remained consistently low from the sixteenth century to the second half of the twentieth. Transnationalization processes in the area of first names are thus a phenomenon peculiar to the twentieth century.

The term transnationalization leaves open the question as to the specific cultural origin of the names parents chose for their children. After 1949 names such as Maurice, Marco, René, Natalie, Denise, Jennifer, Peggy, Sandy, Mike, Marvin, and Steve suddenly gained in popularity. The following figure shows the emergence of first names from Romance (primarily French and Italian) and Anglo-American cultures.

The rise in foreign first names was mainly owing to the increase in names from the Romance and Anglo-American cultural milieus. This was not part of a globalization process proper because the first names came primarily from Western European countries, other foreign cultures being largely neglected.

In terms of first names, transnationalization is above all a process of *occidentalization*, similar to developments in art and science (see Gerhards and Rössel 1999). Interestingly, there was a Westernization of first names not only in West German Gerolstein but in East German Grimma. In East Germany, one might have expected a rise in Slavic and Eastern European names as a result of its being part of

Figure 7.2
Percentage of Romance and Anglo-American Names

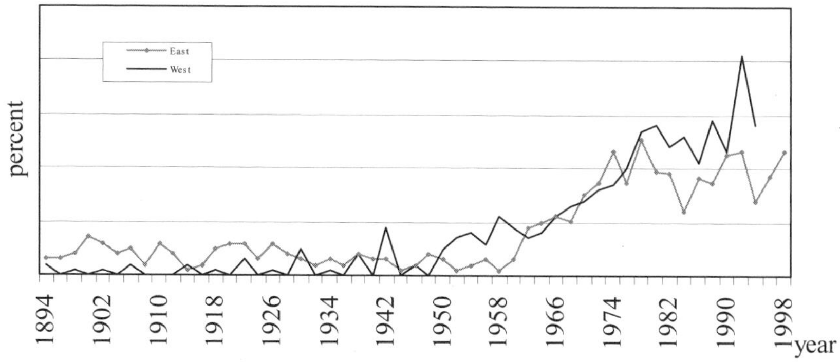

the socialist bloc under Soviet domination. But this had no impact on first names. The publicly propagated solidarity with its socialist brethren in the Eastern bloc did not impress the East German citizenry, who took their cues from the West when it came to naming their children. Horst Naumann, Gerhard Schlimpert, and Johannes Schultheis (1986), Stefan Hornbostel (1997) as well as Michael Wolffsohn and Thomas Brechenmacher (1999) have come to a similar conclusion in their own studies. Neither Ivan nor Bronislaw nor Vladimir nor Nadia nor Tanya were very widespread. Grimma and East Germany as a whole remained Western-oriented and in this respect were no different from West Germany. Although divided in two states, East and West Germany continued to be united in their name preferences.

Also somewhat surprising in view of the large number of Turks immigrating to Germany during this period (Germany's largest group of immigrants), is the fact that Turkish names in West Germany made no headway at all. For example, there were no Mehmets or Mohammeds among those names from other cultures that enjoyed a rise in popularity post-1949.[2]

Causes of the Transnationalization of First Names

The transnationalization of first names at the aggregate level is influenced by several factors whose relative effects I have not been able to determine in a strict methodological sense, but which can be explained by way of empirically founded funded plausibility sketches.

1. The increased popularity of a certain name group always means the decreasing popularity of other name groups. Secularization processes and the discrediting of German names (see chapter 3 and 4) have made room for names from other cultures.

2. It is a safe assumption that children receive names their parents like. The choice of a name from a foreign culture likewise expresses an affinity for that culture. The resort to foreign cultures thus follows a certain social logic, above all when that culture enjoys a certain prestige, that is, has a strong economy. This is confirmed through opinion poll research. Elsewhere in other work I have investigated which foreign groups are most highly esteemed by citizens in twelve countries of the European Union. The analysis showed that Americans and Western Europeans enjoy the greatest prestige, while Eastern Europeans, Turks, Africans, and Asians were much less admired (Fuchs, Gerhards, and Roller 1993). There seems to be a similar trend with regard to foreign names, parents preferring those from western cultures.

3. But in order to choose a previously foreign name, one must first be aware of its existence. How do parents learn of foreign names so that they can even be considered as potential names for their children? There are three hypotheses, one can take into consideration.

First, *they learn of foreign names through immigration into their country.* This is an implausible explanation on several counts. The percentage of Franco-Italian and Anglo-American immigrants into East Germany was minimal. The sharp rise in immigration into West Germany beginning in the 1960s was also not mainly owing to Romance and Anglo-American countries, but to Turks and Yugoslavs,[3] whose influence on first names has been minimal.

Second, *the knowledge of previously foreign names can be traced back to people's foreign travels, which bring them into contact with other cultures.* This is also implausible because even if East Germans traveled more than previously, this travel was largely restricted to Eastern Europe; and Eastern European names were not popular. Travel among West Germans greatly increased as well beginning in the 1950s, but the trips were primarily to Austria, Spain, and Italy, while the increasingly popular names were of Anglo-American and francophone origin.[4]

Third, *an occidentalization of first names can ultimately be traced to the expansion of mass media, primarily television and pop music recordings.* I hold this to be the most plausible of explanations, one that rests on the theory of cultural imperialism. Television was introduced to West Germany in 1954. There was a rapid increase in households with TVs in the space of just a very few years: 1964—55 percent, 1970—85 percent, 1974—95 percent, 1980—97 percent, 1985—97 percent, 1990—98 percent, 1995—98 percent (Berg and Kiefer 1987; 1996). Thus the preconditions were created for receiving information and enjoying entertainment from other countries. The growing popularity of Romance and Anglo-American names and the expansion of television were parallel phenomena. In correlating the number of TV households with the transnationalization index, one arrives at a correlation coefficient of .90.[5] But the increase in television sets does not tell us the content of their programs. A possible measurement of the program content would be to ask from which countries the TV films originate. Foreign names are transmitted via foreign films, and this could have influenced parents' choice of first names. Irmela Schneider (1990: 197) has described the relationship between German and foreign films on German television. The following diagram shows the percentage of non-German, foreign feature films from 1954-1988.[6]

Figure 7.3
Percentage of Foreign Feature Films among Films Shown on the German TV Station ARD

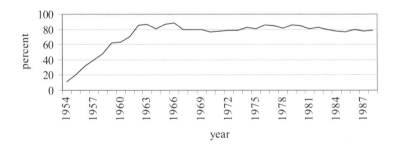

Beginning with the introduction of television sets into Germany there was a rapid rise in the percentage of foreign films shown by ARD, setting the pace for a corresponding rise in transnational names. Here also I have correlated the percentage of foreign films and that of foreign names. The correlation coefficient has a value of .71 (at a significance level of .01).

There was a similar development in theater showings of movies. The market share of foreign films vis-à-vis German ones rose from 51.1 percent in 1955 to 90.7 percent in 1980 (see Bersheim et al. 1999: 87). Irmela Schneider (1990: 194) has shown—as one might expect—that American and British productions were clearly dominant. The next leading countries were France and Italy.

There was a very similar development in the recording industry (records, cassettes, and CDs). The number of recordings sold in Germany as well as in other countries rose exponentially over time (see Beisheim et al. 1999: 96). It is difficult to empirically gauge the correlation between domestic and foreign products and to determine how this relationship—which can be used as an indicator of transnationalization processes in the area of popular culture— changed over time. Andreas Gebesmair (2000) discusses at length the various problems associated with measuring transnational processes and he gives a nice overview of the current state of research. The national origin of a recording or the nationality of its artist is immaterial for our analysis because we are interested in the language in which the song was sung. Moreover, it would be necessary to have information concerning this as well as the charts, both of which are unavailable in any published study. In lieu of that, we must resort to a bit of research that Mattias Hirschfeld (2001) carried out for one of my senior seminars. He evaluated the charts (which were compiled by Media Control for the state association Phono) for the period 1960-2000.[7] On the basis of the song's title and the name of its artist, Hirschfeld grouped the various songs according to their country of origin. Phono states that its data was "the weekly barometer for the German recordings....It encompasses the entire market."[8] The categories which form the basis of this compilation are not exactly clear and neither do they give complete information regarding actual sales, as does Peter Wicke (1996). In my opinion the Media Control charts can nonetheless serve as an indicator for the transnationalization of music, provided one assumes that the data's margin of error remained constant over time. This would mean that although the absolute proportion of German to foreign songs may not be reflected in the data, general trends can indeed be discerned. In grouping the various songs according to language, it emerges that apart from German and English all other languages composed no more than 6 percent of the total.

Figure 7.4
Percentage of Foreign and German Songs in the German Charts (1960-2000)

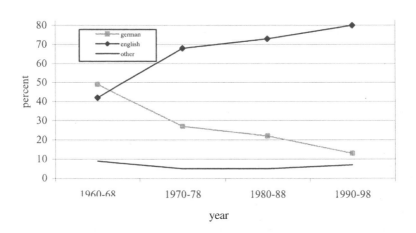

Figure 7.4 shows the percentage of foreign-language songs in the German charts from 1960-2000 (from Hirschfeld 2001). The data has been consolidated into clusters of years because oscillations from one year to the next were rather pronounced. While the percentage of "other languages" hardly changed over time, remaining between 5 percent and 9 percent in any given year, the percentage of German songs declined from 49 percent to 13 percent. At the same time, the percentage of English songs rose from 42 percent to 80 percent. Pop music was undergoing a process of transnationalization, or more precisely, a process of Anglo-Americanization.

Starting in the 1950s the proliferation of television, feature films, and recorded music permitted an exponential rise in German access to the media world and by extension the entertainment industry, which was effecting a transnationalization insofar as the percentage of English and Romance-language products sharply increased in relation to the German-language ones. One can assume that this is how foreign names were transported into the living rooms of German households. John (e.g., Lennon), Steve (e.g., McQueen), Ernie (from "Sesame Street"), Jacqueline (e.g., Kennedy) and Kevin (from the film *Home Alone*, German title: *Kevin allein zu Haus* [Kevin Home Alone]) entered the name repertoire of Germans. These names also originated in cultural milieus that were viewed as prestigious, likely heightening their appeal.

It behooves us to mention two supplementary points regarding transnationalization processes. (1) The western orientation that took place after 1949 in the area of first names went hand in hand with the development of mass communication and popular culture in West Germany. This was no isolated development of the media but was itself imbedded in a process of Western integration after 1945. West Germany was a product of the French, British, and American zones of occupation. The political constitution of the Federal Republic of Germany as a parliamentary democracy; its military integration into NATO and the other western alliance systems; the economic, scholarly, scientific, and artistic orientation toward Europe and America (see Gerhards and Rössel 1999)—all these are symptomatic of West German society's Western orientation after 1949 and the substantial influences on its media and popular culture. (2) The transnationalization of first names and a concrete occidentalization process through the development of mass media also holds for East Germany. The proliferation rate of TV sets was similar to that in West Germany. In 1960, 16 percent of all households in East Germany had televisions; in 1965, 48.5 percent; in 1970, 69.1 percent; in 1981, 90 percent; in 1988, 95.7 percent, thus reaching a saturation point (Geserick 1989: 105). These TVs were not only used to view state-controlled East German television, but West German programs. It is difficult to ascertain just how much West German television was viewed in East Germany (see Linke 1987). By the mid-1970s probably about 80 percent of East Germans could receive the West German station ARD, and in the mid-1980s it was around 90 percent (see Linke 1987: 47). And West German programs were indeed watched. In a survey of the East German Institut für Meinungsforschung, 70 percent of East Germans who owned a TV indicated that they generally preferred West German television (cited in Linke 1987: 48),[9] although certain parts of East Germany could not get West German television—in and around Dresden, the so-called Valley of the Clueless, and in northeastern Mecklenburg. Thus most East Germany citizens had regular access to telecasts and programs of the Federal Republic. East Germans were consequently familiar with the same films and music and actors and singers—and perforce the same Western names.

Let us summarize in theoretical terms why foreign, and above all Western names grew more popular in both East and West Germany starting in the 1950s. From the perspective of parents the choice of a first name is a decision process determined by two factors, namely one's preference for certain names and the known pool of possible names. The transnationalization of first names that took place after the Second World War was owing to the interplay of changed parental preferences and a new name pool. The change in preferences as well as the change in the opportunity structure was strongly influenced by societal change after the Second World War: (a) The discrediting of (mainly) German cultural traditions after the Second World War resulted in German names losing prestige and created the possibility of a change in taste and reorientation that focused on new kinds of names. (b) These new names stemmed from Western societies and cultures that enjoyed high reputations, namely Western ones. (c) But parents could only choose from those names with which they were familiar. The pool of foreign names was first brought to the attention of parents through the development of mass media and its circulation of popular culture. Because popular culture in Germany was primarily of Anglo-American and Romance origin, the range of names to choose among were primarily Anglo-American and Franco-Italian in provenance.

The change in the name pool jibes with the theory of cultural imperialism. On the surface first names would appear to be free of considerations of economic interest because there have never been any businesses in the cultural industry sector that have made a specialty of first names; first names are public goods, they cannot be patented or exploited, and thus there are no industries specializing in their distribution. But our analysis has shown that the transnationalization of the German name pool can be traced back to the growth of television and the pop industry, albeit as an *unintentional byproduct* of these two.

Fashionable Names, Transnational Names, and the Internal Dynamic Contributing to Their Success

Wilfried Seibicke (1996), an expert on German names, deals with a "mechanical process and the motivations that underpin it" (Seibicke 1996: 1207). Seibicke distinguishes between fixed and free names. For Seibicke, fixed names are traditional ones. These might constitute family names or names with religious significance. Only when parents can choose a name outside of traditional parameters do fashionable names arise. "Tradition and fashion are mutually exclusive when it comes to first names; for we can only speak of fashionable names when the dominant or sole paradigm is one of free choice."

(Seibicke 1996: 1212) Like Wilfried Seibecke, Stanley Lieberson (2000: 4) distinguishes between fashion and custom (see also Wilson 1998: 320). A fashion is marked by a change in popular taste. A taste that cannot change because it has been firmly established through social convention and custom, for example a class-defined dress code, is by definition *not* fashion. Accordingly, Lieberson labels any "taste" that refuses to change, a custom. In prior chapters we saw how certain traditions and customs tailed off in the course of the twentieth century, thus paving the way for fashionable first names.

Seibecke (1991) also proposes a method for measuring the dynamics of fashion. The speed at which fashions change is evinced in the number of names squeezed out of the top-ten list from one year to the next and replaced by new ones. Stephen Wilson (1998: 318) and Stanley Lieberson have likewise analyzed the dynamics of fashion by calculating the turnover rate (Lieberson 2000: 36f). I have done the same, tracing the top-ten turnover rate over the past hundred years. For example, if there is no change in the top ten names from 1950 to 1952, then the turnover rate is zero; if two names have changed, the turnover rate is 20 percent. Figure 7.5 shows the results of this analysis.

Figure 7.5
Turnover Rate among the Top Ten Names

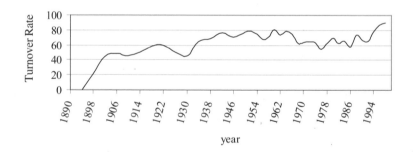

Over time the rate of turnover in both towns rose markedly. Until 1945 the top-ten turnover rate continually increased and then leveled off at a relatively high rate. The tiny fluctuations occurring after 1945 did not lend themselves to any interpretation because they were likely owing to problems with our sample.[10] In fact, what we have here is an accelerated turnover.

With regard to transnationalization we have already seen that as soon as children's names became a matter of fashion Germans seized upon names from Western cultures as a way of being contemporary and distinguishing themselves and their children. But why certain names and not others from the available pool?

In an inductive analysis of first names, Wilfried Seibicke (1977a: 133) ascertained that the popularity of certain names brings other similar-sounding names in their wake. Stanley Lieberson (2000) implicitly piggybacks this idea by asserting that one of the most helpful mechanisms in explaining the internal dynamics of fashion is the "ratchet effect." Every fashionable rejuvenation takes place on the basis of a given structure. At certain points in time people develop certain predilections that manifest themselves in a dominant taste. For example, people wear tight or baggy pants, wear hats or go bareheaded, they listen to rock 'n' roll or hip-hop or they show a preference for French or German names. And most fashionable renewals consist not in a complete overhaul of old fashions but in their moderate makeover; they consist not in a revolution but only in slight changes. The reason is that new things are always evaluated within the framework of the old customs and viewed against their aesthetic criteria (Lieberson 2000: 115). The old preferences create the level of expectations informing recognition and judgment of the new as new. Lieberson leaves open the theoretical question as to why fashion will deviate only incrementally from the old styles. I presume that a mechanism is at work here which learning psychologists' term "incongruence" or "mild discrepancy" (see Trautner 1991: 175 regarding the work of Heinz Heckhausen). The cognitive theory of learning psychology assumes that motivation for learning (and thus for change) is strongest when the new thing to be learned deviates only mildly from what is already familiar. If the deviation is too slight, then there is little motivation to assimilate it; if the deviation is too great, then it cannot be assimilated. The dictates of fashion may well run along similar lines. If the deviation is too small, then something new will not even be understood as new; if it is too great, then there will be no applicable criteria by which to judge it. There must be, as it were, a mild discrepancy between the new fashion and the old.

In his path-breaking analysis of first names, Stanley Lieberson showed that changes in fashion follow precisely this logic,[11] and I am using Lieberson as the basis for my own analysis. The principle of mild deviation on the basis of pre-structuring through an established fashion demonstrates that names will breed others that are phonetically similar. This means that any foreign names introduced into Germany would have to enjoy a certain phonetic similarity to the German ones, while at the same time having a mild discrepancy with the latter which would set them sufficiently apart. One can term this process *creolization*. The success of certain names is owing to the interplay between parental cultural dispositions and the respective exogenous offerings.

Table 7.1 shows how the principal of mild discrepancy can indeed explain the introduction of certain names. In 1970, the name Markus was among the top ten names in Gerolstein and remained there until 1976. In 1974, Marc entered the top ten, as did Marco two years later and remaining for an extended period. In 1992, the French name Marcel broke into the top ten.

Table 7.1
Marcus, Marc, Marco, and Marcel in the Top Ten

	70	72	74	76	78	80	82	84	86	88	90	92
Markus	X	X	X	X					X	X		
Marc			X									
Marco				X		X	X	X				
Marcel												X

Marc, Marco and Marcel are "mutations" of the German name Markus. A similar process took place with Andreas entering the top ten and then the French André following in its wake.

In the following table are two names that are deviations from Stefan. Starting in 1962 Steffen was a perennial top-ten name in Grimma; in 1966 Stefan joined it. In 1978 the English name Steve made it into the top ten—but only after the popularity of Stefan and Steffen had paved the way, and only after the time was ripe for a mild discrepancy.

Table 7.2
Stefan, Steffen, and Steve in the Top Ten

	60	62	64	66	68	70	72	74	76	78
Steffen		X	X	X			X	X		X
Stefan				X		X				X
Steve										X

The logic of mild discrepancy applies not only to male but female names. This is apparent in the following table.

Table 7.3
Female Names in the Top Ten Ending in "y" from 1970 to 1998

	70	72	74	76	78	80	82	84	86	88	90	92	94	96	98
Mandy				X					X	X					
Peggy							X	X							
Cindy									X						
Jenny							X	X			X	X			
Nicky												X			
Emily													X		
Nancy															X

After Mandy broke into Grimma's top ten in 1976 there followed several similar-sounding foreign names. Four years after Mandy came Peggy, six years later came Cindy and Jenny, then Nicky and finally Emily and Nancy.

Jenny, which made the Grimma top ten four times, primed the pump for Jessica in 1990 and Jennifer in 1996.

Even if we have not hereby explained the success of certain foreign names, we have given one answer to the question of how the success of a name contributes to the popularity of like-sounding

Table 7.4
Female Names in the Top Ten Beginning with "J"

	86	88	90	92	94	96	98
Jenny	X	X			X	X	
Jessica			X		X		
Jennifer						X	

names. As a rule, foreign names follow in the slipstream of phonetically similar names that have already firmly established themselves.
The mechanism of mild discrepancy holds true not only for the popularity of certain foreign names but for German or Christian ones as
well. Of course, fashion was a far less powerful dictate in the days
when these were the dominant names. The following table shows
the variations on the root name Chris.

Table 7.5
Male Names in the Top Ten Beginning with Chris

	80	82	84	86	88	90	92	94
Christian		X	X		X		X	
Christopher					X			
Christoph						X		
Chris								X

The success of the name Christian starting in 1982 ushered in first
Christopher, then Christoph, and finally Chris. The data is culled
from Grimma.
Let us summarize our findings. With the establishment of East
and West Germany in 1949 a process of transnationalization set in
with regard to names. Parents increasingly selected names from non-
German cultural spheres, above all Anglo-American and Romance
names, that is, they looked to the West for their cues. At the aggregate level transnationalization processes can be explained through
the interplay of taste and the available name pool. Parents chose

names from those cultures that enjoyed prestigious standing in German society. The discrediting of traditional and principally German names after the Second World War opened the way for other type names to catch on, and this meant those from western cultures whose reputation was high in Germany. Parents, however, could only choose from among those names familiar to them. It was through the growth of mass media and its transmission of popular culture that parents were exposed to foreign names. Because popular culture in Germany was primarily Anglo-American and Franco-Italian, the available pool of names necessarily reflected this.

How do these findings relate to the cultural imperialism theory? Indeed, the transnationalization of names is largely due to media transmission of a popular culture that is mostly of Romance or Anglo-American origin. Names disseminated by the media are those that necessarily condition parental choice. But this is only half the story. Parents only select those names that reflect their personal taste. One can well imagine that in France or in Islamic countries Anglo-American names are far less popular than in Germany, even if Anglo-American popular culture has made similarly vast inroads by way of the media.

The cultural imperialism theory fails to take into account parents' taste, which is conditioned by the culture in which they live. This fact gets pointed out by adherents of the creolization theory when they emphasize that market-distributed products are always adapted to certain criteria of the recipient culture and also enriched by it. Still, these scholars leave open the question as to how exactly this process functions and which mechanisms drive it.

Stanley Lieberson's general theory of fashion has served as the basis by which we have attempted to explain what names are likely to be popular at any given historical moment. According to the principle of mild discrepancy, successful names are those which have phonetic commonalities with the ones currently fashionable. Of all the foreign names from which German parents have been able to choose, only a small portion ever make the top ten. The mechanism at work here is that of mild discrepancy. Popular foreign names are those that are phonetically similar to German ones while at the same time distinguishing themselves through mild discrepancy.

Notes

1. As shown, this does not hold for the process of individuation.
2. By the same token, the adoption of a country's names can serve as an indicator of assimilation. Sasha Weitman (1987) sees children's names between 1882 and 1980 as an indicator for the extent of national and ethnic orientation. Stanley Lieberson (2000: 211) has shown that during the First World War the Jews of Danzig were highly assimilated into German society insofar as they had German names, whereas the Jews in a Polish district near the present-day border with Belarus were largely segregated from their surrounding compatriots insofar as they bore primarily Jewish names.
3. The percentage of foreigners among the total population of West Germany increased at the following rate: 1960—1.2 percent, 1970—4.9 percent, 1975—6.6 percent, 1980—7.2 percent, 1983—7.4 percent, 1985—7.1 percent, 1987—7.6 percent, 1988—7.3 percent, 1990—8.9 percent, 1991—9.8 percent, 1992—10.8 percent, 1993—11.5 percent (see Beisheim et al. 1999: 117).
4. The percentage of foreign trips among total trips by Germans increased at the following rate: 1954—15 percent, 1956—20 percent, 1958—27 percent, 1960—31 percent, 1962—40 percent, 1964—43 percent, 1966—48 percent, 1968—51 percent, 1970—54 percent, 1972—57 percent, 1974—58 percent, 1976—57 percent, 1978—61 percent, 1980—62 percent, 1982—61 percent, 1984—66 percent, 1986—66 percent, 1987—69 percent, 1988—70 percent (see Beisheim et al. 1999: 161).
5. In calculating the correlation coefficient I have only considered the transnational development of names in Gerolstein because statistics on the expansion of television are only for West Germany. As the variable "number of TV households" only has information for a few dates, it was not possible to compute a Cochrane-Orcutt model. Instead, I have made a maximum likelihood estimate: the unstandardized value is 0.4 (with a significance level of 1 percent).
6. Irmela Schneider's "foreign films" (Schneider 1990: 198) consist primarily of American, British, French, and Italian productions. The category of "German films" is composed of West German, East German, and Austrian features. The percentage of foreign films for 1957 was calculated on the basis of the year before and after.
7. Every song in the weekly top twenty received points relative to its position in the charts. Their respective points were then added up for the entire year.
8. Media Central: Kurze Einführung in die offiziellen deutschen Charts; online: http://www.ifpi.de/service/se-charts.htm (song titles in original language).
9. For media developments in the GDR, see also the excellent Master's dissertation of Lars Brücher (2000).
10. I have drawn the ten most popular names from only 100 names per statistical year.
11. In Lieberson's opinion first names are particularly suited to an analysis of changes in taste because they are not fair game for industry marketing strategies as clothes are and because the choice of a certain name depends solely on parental fiat and not on the resources they have at their disposal, which may be class-determined. The external factors thus being neutralized, first names afford a more precise analysis of the internal dynamics of fashion

8

Gender Classification and Changing
Sex Roles

Throughout the twentieth century, and particularly since the 1960s and the women's liberation movement, the rights of women have been gradually expanded. This (hard-won) social change has manifested itself through numerous "hard" and "soft" indicators: the increased percentage of female college students, the greater proportion of working women, the rise in political leadership roles, the changes in divorce and family law as well as general social attitudes toward gender-specific roles.[1] The greater equality of women is also evidenced in the labels used to designate the two sexes. Sole use of the male gender in German has been meantime discredited and largely replaced by male and female forms, for example, *der Präsident* and *die Präsidentin*, or, when possible, through gender-neutral forms of address. For instance, the *Deutscher Soziologentag* (literally: Congress of German [Male] Sociologists) has been changed to the *Deutscher Soziologiekongress* (Congress of German Sociologists), and *Studenten* (the umbrella term for university students both male and female but whose strict grammatical connotation is male) has become *Studierende* (with no specifically male or female connotations). Avoidance of the male form in designating social position or collective subjects is seen as linguistic evidence of a symmetrical and equal valuing of the two sexes.

In this chapter, I will be asking two questions. (1) To what degree are first names used to classify a person's sex and is sex classification by first names becoming more ambiguous over time? (2) If parents choose from different name pools based on the sex of their child, then is this connected with gender-specific roles and how have these changed in the past hundred years?

Demarcating Gender

Gender studies make the conceptual distinction between sex and gender (for a summary see Cerulo 1997). Candice West and Don H. Zimmermann (1991) have expanded this terminological distinction to include a third, namely the "sex category." "Sex" designates the biological sex, the "sex category" is the social construction of male and female, and "gender" indicates male and female role expectations. Sexual classification takes place when a socially defined marker is required to make clear whether we are dealing with a woman or a man (Goffman 1979). Clothes, makeup, hair length, ways of talking and walking can be defined as gender-specific, but they do not have to be, and we can thus speak of socially defined sex classifications.[2] For instance, until recently the wearing of a suit and tie was reserved for men and was a seemingly unambiguous sex marker. In 1970 the German politician Lenelotte von Bothmer created a furor when she became the first woman ever to take the lectern in the German Bundestag in a pantsuit. Vice president of the Bundestag Jäger had declared beforehand that he would allow no woman in pants to appear in plenum, let alone take the lectern. This statement had so incited von Bothmer that she went out and bought a suit with a long jacket and wore it at the very next session of the Bundestag, where she created quite a commotion. She was featured in the press and received endless anonymous letters, many of which were abusive.[3] My sister attended an Ursiline nun Gymnasium in the 1960s where it was prohibited to wear a skirt, but today pants and suits are hardly sexual markers for a person; just look around any university lecture hall or at the latest crop of movies.

One can underscore the sex of babies and children from a very early age. The color blue has traditionally been reserved for boys and pink for girls; dresses and skirts are clear markers for girls and trousers for boys. The following photo, taken in 1911 in Gerolstein, shows very clearly how the sex of the various siblings in a family has been differentiated through hair or lack thereof, ribbons, dresses and posture (girls sitting, boys standing).[4]

Of course, first names can also designate sex. In contrast to marking sex through clothes, however, the marking of sex through names is of greater fundamental importance because it is, as a rule, a lifelong and binary classification applied to all people (Tyrell 1986).[5] But it remains an open question as to whether and to what extent a

first name can indicate the biological sex of a newborn. A comparison of German and American law can help us to answer it.

In Germany, the registry office assesses the legality of names selected by parents for their children. The main consideration is the well-being of the child; legal strictures on parental choice are thus owing to the state's function as public guardian. Impermissible in German law are (a) siblings with the same name; (b) offensive, ludicrous, or otherwise burdensome names as well as those taken from consumer items; and (c) names that are not gender-specific, with certain exceptions such as Maria (see Raschauer 1978; Diederichsen 1995).[6]

The situation is completely different in the USA. Here there are no statutes regulating first names. Anything goes. You can invent new names or use offensive ones or give girls boys' names and vice versa. These legal differences between Germany and America bespeak fundamental cultural ones that are also reflected in other legal issues such as abortion, that is, the stress on individual freedoms versus state regulation in America, and the idea of a paternalistic state in Germany (see Ferree, Gamson, Gerhards, and Rucht 2002). The divergent laws influence the actions of their respective populations by either expanding or limiting their options. Even if application of German law has become less stringent in recent years, the use of gender-neutral names—the use of hitherto female names for boys and male names for girls—is still very limited in comparison to America.

America's liberality in this regard allows an examination of the value parents place on first names as sex markers. Parents draw upon past experience in judging which first names are normally associated with which sex. We know that Peter, Karl, Mike, Thorsten, and Boris are generally boys' names because—either via the media or through our own experience—we have encountered people who bear these names and whose sex we know. As a rule, by dint of past experience, popular names are affiliated in our memories with a certain sex irrespective of whether that affiliation is legally dictated or not. But we cannot draw upon past experience to tell us which names are associated with which sex when we hear a new name. And thus can new names serve in delineating to what extent sex markers are a structuring principle in the bestowal of first names.

Stanley Lieberson and Kelly S. Mikelson (1995) have investigated precisely this question. In contrast to Germany, it is possible in America to invent new names for one's children. Lieberson and Mikelson (1995: 933) took a random sample of eight new boys' names and eight new girls' names in New York state and then asked 225 (relatively) randomly chosen people which were which. I put the Lieberson/Mikelson list of names to a similar test with 184 university students in Leipzig, asking them to distinguish the boys' names from the girls'.

Table 8.1 shows the American and German results. The first column is the original Lieberson/Mikelson list of newly invented names, the second column lists the sex of the so-christened child, and the third and fourth columns show the percentage of right answers among Americans and Germans respectively.

In thirteen of sixteen cases more than half of American respondents were able to correctly identify the name's attributed sex, that is, 81 percent correct answers. Many of the individual names were guessed correctly at a rate of over 80 percent, although 89 percent of respondents classified Chanti as a girl's name as did 75 percent in the case of Furelle, while Kariffe was incorrectly labeled a boy's name by roughly 59 percent of respondents. German respondents answered similarly, with only one or two exceptions.

Because the list consisted of new names, respondents in both countries could not base their answers on personal experience. Characteristic of most of these new names are certain phonemes associated with typically male and female names. In other words, concrete experience with regard to specific names is not the sole prerequisite for recognizing the sex of a given name; a *general phonetic knowledge* can aid in deciphering it as well. And the same phonetic knowl-

Table 8.1
Gender Classification of Newly Invented First Names in the U.S. and Germany

First Name	Sex	Right estimation In the USA	Right estimation In Germany
Lamecca	Weiblich	93,6	97,8
Husan	Männlich	89,5	96,2
Timitra	Weiblich	89,0	94,6
Oukayod	Männlich	86,3	90,2
Maleka	Weiblich	85,5	95,7
Sukoya	Weiblich	79,5	87,0
Jorell	Männlich	79,1	50,0
Rashueen	Männlich	76,4	78,3
Shatrye	Weiblich	72,7	81,5
Gerais	Männlich	71,7	89,1
Triciaan	Weiblich	68,9	7,1
Cagdas	Männlich	68,8	74,5
Shameki	Weiblich	65,5	50,0
Kariffe	Weiblich	41,4	51,1
Furelle	Männlich	25,0	4,3
Chanti	Männlich	10,9	48,3

edge would appear to be shared by Germans and Americans, otherwise it would be impossible to explain the high rate of accordance between the two. That this should be the case is owing to the common linguistic roots of English and German and a shared reservoir of names stemming from military conquest and shared cultural traditions such as Christianity (see Smart 1995).

But what are the distinguishing features of names whose sex can be intelligently guessed at? In their 1995 study, Lieberson and Mikelson explained the answers of the American test persons, and I have adopted their (persuasive) line of argument in attempting to elucidate those of the German respondents. In order to delineate typical phonemes of male and female first names, let us once more examine our Grimma and Gerolstein data. From this pool of names

I have taken those between 1950 and 1990 and analyzed them for gender-specific phonetic characteristics. I am here proceeding on the assumption that gender-specific phonetic characteristics of first names were also implicitly known to the respondents because of their daily interaction with such names. This experience likely formed the basis of the respondents' answers. In determining a typically male or female name one does well to concentrate on the name's ending; if the ending is ambiguous, then the presumption is that one will attempt to derive the name's sex from the other phonemes.[7]

Easiest to explain are the correct answers to names ending in *a*— Lamecca, Timitra, Maleka, and Sukoya. Using our Grimma and Gerolstein data, 95 percent of all names between 1950 and 1990 ending in *a* were feminine; names like Joschka, Joschua and Noah were the exceptions. German parents know this implicitly, and so when they hear a name ending in *a* they assume that it is a girl's name—and as a rule they assume correctly. Female names in English are likewise demarcated through an *a* ending (Lieberson and Mikelson 1995: 936), and this likely explains the similar percentage of correct answers among German and American test persons with regard to names ending in *a*. Most names ending in *e* are also female, although there are exceptions, for example, Ede or Vincente. A name like Shatyre was presumably classified as female due to its *e* ending. The same might be said of Kariffe and Furelle, which were designated female names by the German respondents; in the case of Furelle, falsely.

What the *a* is to female names, the endings *n* and *s* are to male ones. Even if the percentages varied slightly from year to year, over 80 percent of first names between 1950 and 1990 that ended in *n* or *s* were male names. I presume that this implicit background knowledge informed the decision of German test persons in labeling as male the names Husan, Rasshueen, Triciaan, Cagdas and Gerais. Only in the case of Triciaan were they wrong; but they cannot be blamed for this; they were basing their guesses on absolutely correct assumptions regarding names ending in *n* and *s*. Although not to the same extent as names ending in *n* and *s*, our statistics show that names ending in a hard *d* also tended to be those of boys. This might explain why Oukayod was correctly labeled as male by the vast majority of both American and German respondents.

At first glance there is no good explanation for Chanti and Shameki. According to our sample, *i* endings are slightly more frequent in female names but in general the *i* ending is not terribly gender-specific. It is also impossible to judge the name's sex from its beginning. In contrast to American names, the initial sound of *Sh/Ch* (i.e., *Sch*) does not exist among German names. German test persons thus could not fall back on any gender-specific phonemes in assessing these names. This fact may explain why the German respondents were evenly split with regard to both names while the clear majority of Americans cast their vote for them being female.

Stanley Lieberson and Kelly S. Mikelson draw an interesting conclusion from their analysis that is also applicable to Germany (in view of my own replication of their test). Obviously the biological sex of a newborn influences the name-sound combination that parents may find appropriate for their child. Even if parents do not draw from the standard repertoire of names but invent new ones, their choice is structured by the sounds associated with one or the other sex. This implicit knowledge then steers the apparently free decision process in that the child's gender is given a sex marker in the form of a certain first name. A first name as sex marker thus seems also to function under conditions where no legal guidelines regulating the gender-specificity of first names pertain and where there exists no concrete experience as to which first names might be associated with which sex. And as the study of Mikelson and Lieberson shows, inventors of new names as a rule draw on this implicit knowledge and thus mark the sex of the child with the new first name.

As new names cannot be invented under German law, it is impossible to tell whether the above also holds true for Germany and whether a change in sex classifications has taken place over time. But there is another way of testing this. We have seen how there are certain phonemes that are frequently, if not always, assigned to the respective sexes. A change in sex marking through a first name could be, for example, the increasing use of names with phonemes traditionally associated with the opposite sex. The sound of typically female and typically male names is associated with various meanings. Semantic analyses of first names have shown that male names are associated to a larger degree with characteristics such as "strong," "active," and "intelligent," whereas female names are linked to traits like "honest" and "good." (Lieberson and Bell 1992: 539)

In what way might have the preferred phonemes for male and female names developed? Ever since the 1960s women have enjoyed increasing emancipation insofar as the gap between male and female behavior and male and female role expectations has narrowed. The marking out of sex differences has obviously lessened as well. In his analysis of the portrayal of men in print ads in the 1950s, 1970s, and 1990s, Guido Zurstiege (1998) has shown that attractive physical and sexual attributes formerly associated solely with the female sex were gradually integrated into depictions of men. In their analysis of the portrayal of men and women in ads in the German magazine *Stern* from 1969 to 1988, Hans-Bernd Brosius and Joachim F. Staab (1990) have shown that polarized gender roles began slowly to merge. The image of women in advertisements was increasingly modified to incorporate features previously regarded as typically male. One can only assume that there was a parallel androgynous process with respect to first names, that is, sex classification through first names could have decreased over time.

Now, German law prohibits the use of formerly male names for females and the reverse because the sex must be clearly indicated by the name. However, German names may well have become more androgynous over time by virtue of female names having phonemes that were largely typical of male names and vice versa. So as to test this hypothesis, I examined those endings frequently occurring in and largely specific to names of a certain sex. Thus the endings *a* and *e* are classified as female ones and *n*, *s*, *d* and *r* as male phonemes. Then I tested whether there was an increase in boys' names with typically female endings and whether there was an increase in girls' names with typically male endings.

Figure 8.1
Gender-Specific Endings from 1950 to 1990

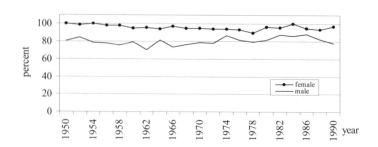

Figure 8.1 shows the result of this analysis. The percentage of female endings was mostly just under 100 percent and the male endings were roughly 80-90 percent. In the 1970s and 1980s there occurred a very slight decrease in gender-specific phonemes, but the percentages for 1990 and 1950 are virtually the same.

The result of our analysis is relatively clear. Names were no more androgynous in 1990 than they were in 1950. Classifying a child's sex through the first name has not changed over the years. This finding is supported by the evidence of Stanley Lieberson, Susan Dumais, and Shyon Baumann (2000) for the USA. Because in America one cannot necessarily know the sex of a person from their first name, Lieberson et al. required a different form for measuring greater androgyny in names. They investigated to what extent first names were restricted to one sex and whether or not there had been any change over time. "97 percent of names are given to children of the same gender. The second important feature of figure 1 is the absence of any obvious trend through the years." (Lieberson, Dumais and Baumann 2000: 1261).[1]

Let us summarize our findings. The classification of children according to sex by way of first names is in principle an open process, but in reality, in both America and Germany, completely structured. We have seen that even when parents invent names instead of resorting to a standard repertoire, their decision is largely structured by those phonemes typically associated with male and female names. This implicit knowledge allows people to know the sex of a child solely through its name. Such sex classification appears to remain stable even under conditions in which other sex markers (fashion) have changed and gender role expectations have narrowed. We have seen that the unambiguity of phonetic sex markers has not changed over time (1950-1990). It would appear that the categorization of sex through names is based on such a fundamental regulatory mechanism that it remains unaffected by any change in gender roles or any differences that might exist between Germany and America. This seems also to be the case with regard to the classification of sex according to voice and visual perception. Monique Biemans (1999) has shown that people draw strong correlations between a person's voice and stereotypical male and female characteristics (see also Strand 1999) and Kristi Lemm and Mahzarin R. Banaji (1999) have shown that unconscious sex stereotypes inform people's classification of others. These findings support the system-theory argument of Hartmann Tyrell, who asserts that sex classification is all about a particular form of binary coding. However, it remains an open question as to whether it is also a universal form of classification that plays a fundamental role in all societies.

Cultural Change and Sex Roles

In the foregoing chapters we have shown that first names are good indicators for the analysis of processes of cultural change. We could, for example, show that over the past hundred years there has been an increasing secularization and a concomitant decrease in the importance of family traditions, and that a process of individuation and cultural transnationalization has taken place. In the following we want to test whether there have been gender-specific differences involved in the various processes of cultural modernization, and if so, how these can be properly understood. We will be moving away from an analysis of sex categorization and to one concerning the definition of gender roles through first names.

For this analysis I have placed first names into three cultural categories. The first two are the traditional ones—Christian and German—and the third is the transnational category, including all foreign cultures (Anglo-American, Eastern European, Latin, etc.). Our analysis will encompass the period from 1894 to 1994. By the end of the nineteenth century, the pool of names at the disposal of parents was doubly limited insofar as the total number of names was small (many children in a community bearing the same name) and names for both sexes were generally drawn solely from the German and Christian traditions.

Figure 8.2 shows the percentage of German/Christian names as well as the percentage of foreign names for boys and girls respectively.

At the end of the nineteenth century about 85 percent of names per annum were German or Christian. This percentage remained relatively stable for both sexes until the establishment of East and West Germany. Then the course of things changed rapidly insofar as names from other cultural milieus were increasingly used, something that we examined in chapter 7. The greater openness to foreign cultures began earlier with girls' names than with boys', and at a significantly higher level. The readiness to utilize names from foreign cultures rose generally, but the boys' names remained more *traditional*. The tendency of female names to be more fashionable is witnessed in a second indicator (see also Seibicke 191: 100). I have calcu-

Figure 8.2
Gender and the Decreasing Importance of Tradition

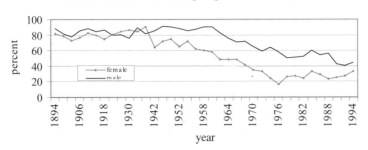

lated the top-ten turnover rate for male and female names separately, and the rate for female names is clearly higher, that is, they are trendier. Evidently tradition weighs more heavily in the balance when parents go about selecting a name for their male scions, whereas they are more prepared to experiment with new names from other cultures—which they have likely accessed through the media—when they set about naming a girl. More traditional names for boys and more fashionable (foreign) ones for girls express gender-specific attitudes. Whereas boys are beholden to notions of "permanence" and "stability," girls are less freighted with these expectations and can safely bear names that would appear more evanescent and ephemeral; one finds parallels to this in fashion as well. This interpretation is supported by the findings of other researchers (see Mitterauer 1988; 1993).

But let us take a closer look at what "traditional" means for each sex. In figure 8.2 we saw that the percentage of Christian and German names *taken together* among boys and girls over the past hundred years was disproportionate. Let us now examine Christian and German names separately. We might recall that religious attitudes are manifested in the bestowal of Christian names and particularly in those of Christian saints.

Figure 8.3 shows that there was a decrease in Christian names for boys until 1950 and for girls until 1970. It shows also that the percentage of Christian names among girls was higher than for boys until about 1970, at which point the former leveled off at 20 percent while the latter rose to 30 percent.

These gender-specific differences in the area of Christian names can be better interpreted if one also takes into account German names, the second traditional source of names. Figure 8.4 shows the percentages of German names from 1894 to 1994 for boys and girls.

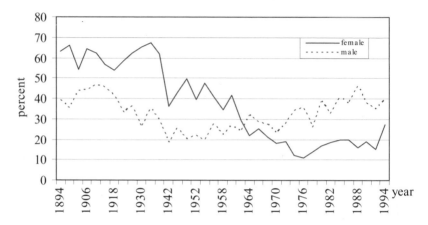

Figure 8.3
Percentage of Christian Names for Boys and Girls

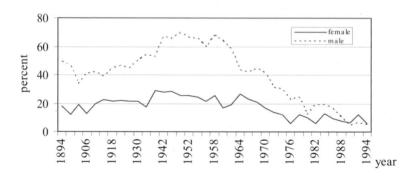

Figure 8.4
Percentage of German Names for Boys and Girls

The percentage of German names among males is much higher than that among females, and the percentage of German names among the populace as a whole is largely owing to males. While parents tended to give German names to boys, they ordinarily gave Christian names to girls. This expressed certain gender-specific attitudes. Whereas boys were affiliated with an active life in service of German-national ideals, girls were restricted to an ethereal sphere detached from the physical world. These cultural connotations were a product of their historical time.

In the course of the nineteenth century and especially with the founding of the Kaiserreich in 1871, German nationalism became more radicalized. In chapter 3 we saw how the increase in nationalism stood in a causal relationship to the increase in German names. German historiography has sometimes shortchanged the fact that formation of the German nation in general and construction of German history in particular has been primarily a process directed by and for males.[2] The process of nation building was first and foremost aimed at men: politics and the public sphere were seen as a male domain. Women were largely excluded from this process just as they were excluded from voting and that "school of the nation," the military. George Mosse (1997) has attempted to show that the construction of masculinity and the linking of these ideals with the idea of the nation and the resuscitation of national ideals was not only a German phenomenon. This German-national mobilization of males reached its high point in the First World War and encompassed also Catholics and workers, two groupings that had shown some resistance to German nationalism hitherto.[3]

Boys' names are to be seen in this context. The resort to German names was part and parcel of the "invention of tradition" (Hobsbawm 1984), and Germanness was primarily associated with a strengthening of the male domain. This found its expression in names, with boys receiving German names and girls receiving religious names that had greater spiritual connotations.[4]

As in other spheres, the Nazis seized upon this masculine tradition and pushed it to extremes. "Never before and never thereafter was masculinity raised to such heights as during the period of fascism; every fascist regime placed great hopes in it, and made it into a national symbol and an aspirational goal" (Mosse 1996). The success of the Nazis' German-national masculine ideology was also evinced in a continued and dramatic rise in popularity of German names after 1933, and this primarily among boys. The groundwork for this development was laid by the Kaiserreich and given a fillip by the First World War. The extraordinary increase in male German names under the Nazis was merely the end result of a self-consciously masculine style of nationalism that emerged ever more strongly after 1871 and helped define name-giving parameters for the next few generations.

Women were only partly included in this process. Their realm was spiritual and private to the same degree that the male sphere was national and public. In the nineteenth century, in both the Protestant and Catholic churches, there was growing participation of women in religious activities (von Olenhausen 1995; Busch 1995; McLeod 1988). There was not only an increase in female church attendance and female communicants, but an increase in female religious orders and church associations such as the Herz-Jesu Verein. This "feminization" of both the Protestant and Catholic religions influenced the process of name-giving insofar as Christian names for girls increased.

As we have shown in previous chapters, there were processes of change that applied equally to both sexes, namely traditional culture lessening in influence as individualism increased and foreign cultural milieus acquired greater cachet. At the same time there were gender-specific differences. Boys' names remained more traditional whereas girls names were more susceptible to change and foreign influence. "Traditional" also meant different things for each sex. Boys' names were largely traditional German ones and reflected the rise in German nationalism, while girls' names drew on the Christian tradition. Both findings indicate that first names were closely connected with typical views of gender roles that have seen little change over the years.

When we combine this finding with that from the first part of this chapter, we emerge with a consistent if somewhat surprising result. First names have shown themselves to be a fundamental mechanism in classifying sex that is unaffected by social change. Whereas there has certainly been change with regard to the influx of foreign names, the gender-specific connotations of first names have remained. While gender roles may have changed in many areas of society, gender-specific names have proven resistant to these socially transforming processes.

Notes

1.   See the statistical information in the "Datenreport des Statistischen Bundesamtes" (2000: 73, 88, 516); for an overview see Gertrud Nunner-Winkler (2001).
2.   For a good current overview of this subject as well as a collection of empirical studies, see the anthology edited by Ursula Pasero and Friederike Braun (1999).
3.   One letter stated, "Poor Germany! To what depths you have sunk with these red party women!" (Bothmer 1996)

4.   The photo shows children of the Breuer family and is from the volume *Gerolstein in alten Ansichten*, ed. P. Josef Böffgen.

5.   Hartmann Tyrell (1986) applied the Luhmann code theory to the classification of sex in order to demonstrate the unlikeliness and preconditions of a binary coding.

6.   German law stipulates that anyone undergoing a sex change must also undertake a name change.

7.   This has also proven itself in the practice of registry offices and name consultants. Wilfried Seibicke (1991: 260) finds that a list of first names arranged alphabetically according to the last letter (and working backward) is helpful in determining a name's gender.

11.   The study of Herbert Barry III and Aylene S. Harper (1993) arrives at another result for the USA. However, the authors' method has been justifiably criticized (see Lieberson, Dumais, and Baumann 2000: 1257).

12.   For example, this aspect goes begging in the voluminous and otherwise outstanding social history of Hans-Ulrich Wehler.

13.   Specific events and persons are also reflected in specific names. Michael Wolffsohn and Thomas Brechemacher (1999: 190) have shown how the name Wilhelm was popular during German successes in the first part of the First World War, but that it was no longer so with the impending and subsequent defeat of Germany. The authors thus draw the conclusion—a not unreasonable one, I think— that Wilhelm II was in large part the inspiration for parents naming a son Wilhelm.

14.   In her analysis of first names at the time of the French Revolution, Nicoline Hörsch (1994) has arrived at a similar gender-specific finding: 66 percent of republican names were for men and 34 percent for women.

9

Synopsis: Cultural Developments and First Names

The basic assumption of sociology is that human behavior is to a large degree influenced by the social conditions in which people are embedded. This sociological view of the world was most forcefully formulated by Émile Durkheim.

A child's first name is, of course, a free and private decision of the parents, and at first glance there would seem to be very little social influence involved. But as Niklas Luhmann (1981: 170) has stressed, sociology is not a discipline of first glances. Accordingly, we began with the assumption that even a supposedly private and idiosyncratic parental decision regarding a child's name is largely subject to social structuring; we wished to show how one's social context can have an impact on just such a private decision and how first names can thus serve as social indicators. Indicators are empirical "markers" that point to the existence of facts that were theoretically assumed. In this study we have utilized first names as indicators for measuring processes of cultural change from the end of the nineteenth to the end of the twentieth century. Our leading assumption throughout has been that macro-cultural developments are reflected in the micro-phenomenon of name giving.

Ever since the "cultural turn," studies of culture have enjoyed enormous popularity in the social sciences and humanities. But as I stated in the first chapter, I find the premises of the cultural turn and its consequences for research unpersuasive. Our analysis of first names was partly intended to show that the classic instruments of sociology and its scientific theoretical grounds are still useful in an analysis of cultural change within society.

What findings have we made, what trends have we ascertained, and how can these be explained? We have subsumed several theories under the rubric of social change. Starting point for our analysis of cultural development has been collective and group-specific definitions of meaning (religion, nation, family, class) whose importance has decreased over the years. At one time religion did indeed form a mainstay of personal meaning and was a filter through which everyday phenomena were viewed. We have seen how in the twentieth century distinct secularization processes were at work in the area of names: the percentage of Christian names from the Bible and inspired by saints receded over time, and names in general became less "transcendent."

Any explanation of secularization processes must take into account several causes. For one, modernization processes that have markedly improved the welfare and security of people and raised their educational level, have also reduced people's demand for religious orientation and increased criticism of "God-given" commandments. We were also able to show that one must consider the strategies and world-views of religion's "supply side" as well as its secular competitors. Our empirical analyses have demonstrated that the ascertainable differences between Protestants and Catholics in the area of Christian first names are explicable only in light of the differing attitudes brought about by the Reformation and Counter-Reformation and their respective church politics. Lastly, and in particular after 1933, Christian names once more demonstrated that it is insufficient to examine solely the religious providers but that one must also include the strategies of competitive secular worldviews. For the decline in Christian names after post-1933 was obviously the result of Nazi ideology, which succeeded in persuading parents to give their newborns German names rather than Christian ones.

German names are the second traditional source from which parents draw. In our analysis of German names we focused on how they linked up with political developments. We were able to show that the rise of nationalism in the nineteenth century led to the greater popularity of German names, a popularity that was maintained up until 1945 and the collapse of the Third Reich. The construction of a nation also consists of the construction of a common past. In any construction of a shared history there are seminal figures who helped to shape that history. The building of a German national consciousness was thus accompanied by the construction of a history of great Germans who were seen as having strengthened the nation, and it were precisely these historical ancestors who served as namesakes for newborns. The discrediting of nationalism through German defeat in the Second World War and the downfall of National Socialism had its counterpart in the decreasing popularity of German names. Both successor states of the Third Reich—the Federal Republic of Germany and the German Democratic Republic—not only abandoned traditional definitions of national identity but helped to discredit them. This discrediting of German traditions was reflected in a radical curtailment in the popularity of German names post-1945.

Family and relatives are the third traditional ligature of integration and the creation of meaning. Kith and kin structures find their expression in numerous ways, among these being first names. To pass down the names of grandparents and parents can be interpreted as the attempt to place the newborn child in the family line and thereby express the importance of family traditions. In our study we have proceeded on the assumption that over time there has been a diminishing effort to bind children to the family line through transmission of family traditions, and our analysis has borne that out. The integration of one's progeny in the family line appears to have become less important to parents over time, for traditional family names are being passed down less and less. We have explained this development as a result of the decreasing economic dependence between parents and children. The more parents and children are economically independent of one another, the lower the percentage of names that are passed on from one generation to the next. The independence of children from their parents has been the result of two social-structural changes, namely the increase in gainful employment outside of the parental home (as opposed to working on the family farm), and the expansion of the social welfare system in place of family solidarity. Both of these factors have loosened family ties and made integration of children into the family line less imperative.

Religion, nation and family together form the traditional ligatures of the creation of meaning and the structuring of behavior. But when these points of reference lessen in significance, what is there to take their place? Ralf Dahrendorf believes it likely that the breaking up of traditional ties is the precondition for individual emancipation. Both Georg Simmel and Ulrich Beck speak of a process of increasing individuation. Individuation as a concept for designating a feature of modernization means that people share fewer and fewer characteristics with their fellow humans and thus become increasingly different from one another. Individuality can manifest itself in a variety of ways, and first names are among these. The fewer people who bear the same name, the more they emerge as distinct units and thus as individuals. We have been able to show that in the course of the twentieth century people have in fact become increasingly individuated. Whereas in 1894, 34 percent of names were different, one hundred years later 81 percent were (a level that had been essentially reached by the early 1950s).

Classic sociology originally traced the individuation process back to the increasing division of labor. The rise in the number of work activities and roles made a person into a unique individual because he alone occupied a certain point at the intersection of a concatenation of social circles. And our empirical analysis has indeed shown that the individuation of first names was accompanied by an increase in occupational differentiation.

The decreasing importance of the two cultural traditions, the German and the Christian, allowed for the incursion of foreign names. We have interpreted the greater openness toward foreign cultures as a transnationalization process, and as a matter of fact, after the Second World War there was an enormous increase in foreign names among German children. This development was due primarily to the sudden popularity of names from Romance and Anglo-American cultures. This was not a globalization process in the true sense because these names stemmed mostly from Western European nations, whereas other cultures—for example, the highly conspicuous Turkish culture—were largely passed over. For not all available names are equally attractive to parents; they choose names from those cultures that enjoy a high societal standing. Transnationalization in the area of names was first and foremost a Westernization process, and, interestingly enough, one that applied to both East and West Germany. From the standpoint of first names, the attempt to integrate the German Democratic Republic into the Eastern bloc was a complete failure. East German citizens looked westward for their monikers.

We have traced the transnationalization of first names to the expansion and westernization of TV, film, and the music industry. For parallel to this process was the rise of both East and West German households that had access to the media world with its mainly English-language products. Thus were foreign names ushered into German living rooms and subsequently bestowed on German children.

But from among the numerous foreign and mostly western names, only a portion have ever made it into the German top ten. In the attempt to explain which of the first names or which type of first names possess higher chances of success, we have employed general theories of fashionability. According to the principle of mild discrepancy it is likely that those first names are successful which have phonetic similarities to names currently in fashion; thus, certain foreign names are popular because they are different from German names while yet still sharing particular phonemes. Generally speaking, the diffusion of transnational names operates in three stages: (1) greater variation in the name pool through expansion and westernization of media offerings; (2) name selection based on the reputation of certain cultural milieus; and (3) selection on the basis of phonetic similarities to native names.

We have not only examined names over the past one hundred years in aggregate, but simultaneously analyzed our data along class and gender-specific lines. First names can be interpreted as a parental expression of taste that always has the function of social classification. By giving a child a particular name, parents tell the world (and themselves) to which stratum they feel akin. One can therefore presume that names vary according to class and serve consciously or unconsciously as status markers. An examination of names over the past hundred years betrays no diminution of this function but rather an increase in class-specific names. This held true not only for West Germany but for East Germany as well. The "classless society" of the German Democratic Republic did not translate into a homogenization of first names.

Equally resistant to change were gender-specific differences in names. The classification of a newborn as male or female by virtue of their name is in principle an open, socially constructed act; but underlying is the fact that even when parents do not draw from a standard repertoire of names but invent new ones, these are largely structured by gender specific phonemes. This implicit knowledge leads to the first name serving as a sex classifier for third parties, and the unambiguity of these phonetic markers has not changed over time.

There has also been little change with regard to the gender-role associations of names. Boys' names are more traditional, whereas girls' names are more susceptible to change and are more likely to be of foreign origin. Moreover, "tradition" has different connotations for each sex. While boys' names are predominantly from the German tradition and reflect the popularity of a masculine style of German nationalism, girls' names stem from the Christian tradition and have ethereal, religious overtones. These findings would indicate that first names are closely linked with gender-specific role expectations and that in this regard there has been little change over the past century. Whereas gender roles have altered in many areas of society, the gender-specific connotations of first names have proven solidly resistant to change.

Let us examine once more the various factors behind cultural modernization with regard to first names. (a) Changes in the social structure were of decisive importance. Increased prosperity and education laid the groundwork for secularization processes; industrialization (breakdown of the primary sector) and growth of the welfare state led to the family's decreasing importance; and a differentiated occupational structure promoted individuation processes. (b) The political system emerged as a significant factor. Its nationalist orientation informed the turn toward German traditions beginning in the nineteenth century, then after 1945 its greater receptivity to the west helped usher in foreign names. (c) Finally, we have seen that collective actors and a particular constellation of actors can modify processes that emanate from social-structural conditions. We were able to see this primarily in church politics: (1) social-structural modernization leading to secularization processes was only possible with the religious market being dominated by the two official churches, and (2) nationalism was clearly promoted through the alliance between the Protestant church and the nation-state.

If the social conditions created by these three factors change, this will have consequences for parental choices with regard to names. Social frameworks set the parameters within which parents make their selections, and when these parameters change then parental behavior and decision-making is necessarily affected. Macro-conditions can indeed be linked up to individual decision-making processes. At the same time, I seriously doubt whether one can reconstruct macro-societal trends by relying on empirical studies of the motives, preferences and perceived restrictions of parents. As a supplement to this study we undertook a small survey of parents in a post-natal ward so as to learn why they chose a certain name for their child (see Gerhards and Hackenbroch 1997). In contrast to the registry office data which lent itself to interpretation by classic theories of cultural change and yielded clear structural lines of development, in the post-natal survey almost half of all parents could give no clear reasons for their choice of first name, and even the proffered explanations were often rather vague. This contrast between clear social patterns and vague parental reasoning would lead one to conclude that society's impact is decisive even when people are unaware of it.

And finally, a prognosis. What will be the developmental trends of the future? Our analysis has shown that over the past hundred years first names broke free from the traditions of religion, family and the nation, and that this had structural causes. Only after the weakening of these traditions did first names become susceptible to fashionable trends. Thus, we can only assume that the dynamics of fashion will continue to spearhead developments in the future.

Fashion is driven by the need for distinction and self-definition in opposition to the status quo. Stanley Lieberson (2000) has already done fine work in this area. Every fashion takes shape in contradistinction to the status quo. Because the reservoir of first names is limited—despite its expansion through transnationalization processes—distinction can be won, among other things, through recourse to old names. This, however, is only the case after elapse of a large span of time. Only after a previous fashion has been forgotten can it be reintroduced as a new one and impart the necessary distinction. This is the (extended) cyclic nature of fashion.

What does all this mean for the future of first names? Fashionable trends will dictate first a wave of foreign names that will eventually subside and then be followed by a wave of traditional Christian and German names—but only after these have lost their original connotations and/or been forgotten. This already seems to be the case for Christian names; I presume that we will also soon witness a new wave of German names. Then Karl, Heinrich, Wilhelm, Otto, Berta, Erna, and Annegret will once more be in the top ten and have replaced Leon, Daniel, Niklas, Sophie, Michelle, Sarah, and Hannah until the day when—after a long period of latency—these once more will have their chance.

References

Ahlbrecht, Heinz and Andreas Letzner, 1988: Die Vornamen der Berliner heute und im historischen Vergleich, in: *Berliner Statistik* 42: 174-212.

Alexander, Jeffrey, 1987: Lecture One: What is a Theory? Pp. 1-21 in: *Twenty Lectures: Sociological Theory*. New York.

Alexander, Jeffrey, 1988: The new theoretical movement. Pp. 77-101 in: Neil Smelser (ed.), *Handbook of Sociology*. Beverly Hills: Sage.

Alford, Richard D., 1988: *Naming and Identity: A Cross-cultural Study of Personal Naming Practices*. New Haven, Connecticut: HRAF Press.

Allen, L., V. Brown, L. Dickinson, and K. C. Pratt, 1941: The Relation of First Name Preferences to their Frequency in the Culture, in: *Journal of Social Psychology* 14: 279-293.

Ambrosius, Gerald and Hartmut Kaelble, 1992: Einleitung: Gesellschaftliche und wirtschaftliche Folgen des Booms der 1950er und 1960er Jahre. Pp. 8-32 in: Hartmut Kaelble (ed.), *Der Boom 1948-1973. Gesellschaftliche und wirtschaftliche Folgen in der Bundesrepublik Deutschland und in Europa*. Opladen: Westdeutscher Verlag.

Aron, Raymond, 1979: Emile Durkheim. Pp. 19-95 in: Raymond Aron, *Hauptströmungen des soziologischen Denkens. Durkheim - Pareto - Weber*. Reinbek: Rowohlt.

Andersen, Christian, 1977: *Studien zur Namengebung in Nordfriesland. Die Bökingharde 1760-1970*. Clausthal-Zellerfeld: Böneke.

Bahr, Howard M., Jean-Hugues Déchaux, and Karin Stiehr, 1994: The Changing Bonds of Kinship: Parents and Adult Children. Pp. 115-171 in: Simon Langlois (ed.): *Convergence or Divergence? Comparing Recent Social Trends in Industrial Societies*. Frankfurt a. M.: Campus.

Barber, Benjamin, 1996, *Coca Cola und Heiliger Krieg*. Bern: Scherz.

Barry III, Herbert and Aylene S. Harper, 1993: Feminization of Unisex Names from 1960 to 1990, in: *Names* 41: 228-238.

Barry III, Herbert and Aylene S. Harper, 1998: Phonetic Differentiation between First Names of Boys and Girls. Pp. 40-46 in: *Proceedings of the XIXth International Congress of Onomastic Sciences*. University of Aberdeen.

Beck, Ulrich, 1983: Jenseits von Stand und Klasse? Pp. 35-74 in: Reinhard Kreckel (ed.): *Soziale Ungleichheiten*. Göttingen: Schwartz.

Beck, Ulrich, 1986: *Risikogesellschaft. Auf dem Weg in eine andere Moderne*. Frankfurt a. M.: Suhrkamp.

Beck, Ulrich, 1995: Die »Individualisierungsdebatte." Pp. 185-198 in: Bernhard Schäfers (ed.), *Soziologie in Deutschland. Entwicklung, Institutionalisierung und Berufsfelder. Theoretische Kontroversen*. Opladen: Leske und Budrich.

Beck, Ulrich and Elisabeth Beck-Gernsheim, 1993: Nicht Autonomie, sondern Bastelbiographie. Anmerkungen zur Individualisierungsdiskussion am Beispiel des Aufsatzes von Günter Burkhart, in: *Zeitschrift für Soziologie* 22: 178-187.

Beck, Ulrich and Elisabeth Beck-Gernsheim, 1995: Individualisierung in modernen Gesellschaften – Perspektiven und Kontroversen einer subjektorientierten Soziologie. Pp. 10-39 in: Ulrich Beck and Elisabeth Beck-Gernsheim (eds.), *Riskante Freiheiten*. Frankfurt a. M.: Suhrkamp.

Beck, Ulrich and Ulrich Sopp (eds.), 1997: *Individualisierung und Integration. Neue Konfliktlinien und neuer Integrationsmodus?* Opladen: Leske und Budrich.

Beck-Gernsheim, Elisabeth, 2002: Namenspolitik: Zwischen Assimilation und Antisemitismus – zur Geschichte jüdischer Namen im 19. und 20. Jahrhundert, in: Armin Nassehi and Markus Schroer (eds.), *Der Begriff des Politischen. Sonderheft der Sozialen Welt.* Baden Baden: Nomos.

Becker, Nikolas, 1983: Hans und Grete, Momo und Azalee. Namenwahl als Zeitgeschichte, in: *Kursbuch* 72: 154-165.

Beisheim, Marianne, Sabine Dreher, Gregor Walter, Bernhard Zangl, and Michael Zürn, 1999: *Im Zeitalter der Globalisierung? Thesen und Daten zur gesellschaftlichen und politischen Denationalisierung.* Baden-Baden: Nomos.

Berg, Klaus and Marie Luise Kiefer (eds.), 1987: *Massenkommunikation: eine Langzeitstudie zur Mediennutzung und Medienbewertung*, Vol. 3. Frankfurt a. M./ Berlin: Metzner.

Berg, Klaus and Marie Luise Kiefer (eds.), 1996: *Massenkommunikation V. Eine Langzeitstudie zur Mediennutzung und Medienbewertung 1964-1995*, Baden-Baden: Nomos.

Berger, Hans, 1967: *Volkskundlich-soziologische Aspekte der Namensgebung in Frutingen (Berner Oberland).* Bern: Verlag Paul Haupt.

Berger, Peter A., 1996: *Individualisierung. Statusunsicherheit und Erfahrungsvielfalt.* Opladen: Westdeutscher Verlag.

Berger, Peter A., 1997: Individualisierung und sozialstrukturelle Dynamik. Pp. 81-98 in Ulrich Beck and Peter Sopp (eds.), *Individualisierung und Integration. Neue Konfliktlinien und neuer Integrationsmodus.* Opladen: Leske und Budrich.

Berger, Peter, 1973: *Zur Dialektik von Religion und Gesellschaft. Elemente einer soziologischen Theorie.* Frankfurt a. M.: Fischer.

Bering, Dietz, 1987/1992: *Der Name als Stigma. Antisemitismus im Deutschen Alltag 1812-1933.* Stuttgart: Klett-Cotta.

Bering, Dietz, 1992: *Kampf um Namen: Bernhard Weiss gegen Joseph Goebbels.* Stuttgart: Klett-Cotta.

Bertram, Hans, 1995: Individuen in einer individualisierten Gesellschaft. Pp. 9-34 in: Hans Bertram (ed.), *Das Individuum und seine Familie. Lebensformen, Familienbeziehungen und Lebensereignisse im Erwachsenenalter.* Opladen: Leske und Budrich.

Besnard, Philippe, 1991: Le choix d'un prénom. Actualité de la méthode durkheimienne, in : *Recherches Sociologiques* 22: 53-60.

Besnard, Philippe, 1994: A Durkheimian Approach to the Study of Fashion: The Sociology of First Names' in: W.S.F. Pickering and H. Martins (eds.): *Debating Durkheim*, London: Routledge.

Besnard, Philippe, 1995: The Study of Social Taste Through First Names: Comment on Lieberson and Bell, in: *American Journal of Sociology* 100: 1313-1317.

Besnard, Philippe and Desplanques, Guy, 1986: *Un prénom pour toujours: La cote des Prénoms*, Paris: Balland.

Besnard, Philippe and Grange, Cyril, 1993: La fin de la diffusion verticale des gouts? (Prénoms de l'élite et du vulgum), in: *L'Année sociologique* 43: 269-294.

Biemans, Monique, 1999: Production and perception of gendered voice quality. Pp. 63-72 in: Ursula Pasero and Friederike Braun (eds.), *Wahrnehmung und Herstellung von Geschlecht.* Opladen: Westdeutscher Verlag.

Bieritz, Karl-Heinz, 1991: *Das Kirchenjahr. Feste, Gedenk- und Feiertage in Geschichte und Gegenwart.* München: Beck.

Blau, Peter M., 1994: *Structural Contexts of Opportunities*, Chicago and London: University of Chicago Press.

Block, Eva, 1984: Freedom, Equality, Et Cetera. Values and Valuations in the Swedish Domestic Political Debate 1954-1975. Pp. 159-166 in: Gabriele Melischek, Karl Erik Rosengren and James Stappers (eds.), *Cultural Indicators: An International Symposium*. Wien: Verlag der österreichischen Akademie der Wissenschaften.

Blossfeld, Hans-Peter, 1985: *Bildungsexpansion und Berufschancen. Empirische Analysen zur Lage der Berufsanfänger in der Bundesrepublik*. Frankfurt a. M./New York: Campus.

Bohrhardt, Ralf, and Wolfgang Voges, 1995: Die Variable ›Beruf‹ in der empirischen Haushalts- und Familienforschung. Zur Ausschöpfung relevanter Informationsanteile aus standardisierten Berufsklassifikationssystemen, in: *ZA-Information* 36: 91-113.

Bosshart, Louis, 1973: Motive der Vornamengebung im Kanton Schaffhausen von 1960-1970. Dissertation. Universität Freiburg (Schweiz).

von Bothmer, Lenelotte, 1996: *"Mit der Kuh am Strick" Szenen aus den Dienstjahren einer Hinterbänklerin*. Hamburg: Antonia Verlag.

Bourdieu, Pierre, 1982: *Die feinen Unterschiede. Kritik der gesellschaftlichen* Urteilskraft. Frankfurt a. M.: Suhrkamp.

Breuilly, John, 1999: *Nationalismus und moderner Staat. Deutschland und Europa. Übersetzt und herausgegeben von Johannes Müller*. Köln: SH-Verlag.

Brosius, Hans-Bernd and Joachim F. Staab, 1990: Emanzipation in der Werbung? Die Darstellung von Frauen und Männern in der Anzeigenwerbung des "Stern" von 1969 bis 1988, in: *Publizisitik* 35: 292-303.

Brücher, Lars, 2000: Das Westfernsehen und der revolutionäre Umbruch in der DDR im Herbst 1989. Master's dissertation, Department of History, University of Bielefeld. http://www.lars-bruecher.de/ddr_westmedien.htm.

Buch, Dieter, 1974: Die Vornamen der Hamburger, in: *Hamburg in Zahlen*, Heft 9: 284-288.

Buch, Dieter and Klaus Kamp, 1984: Die häufigsten Vornamen der Hamburger Kinder, in: *Hamburg in Zahlen*, Vol. 4: 110-111.

Buchmann, Marlis and Manuel Eisner, 2001: Geschlechterdifferenzen in der gesellschaftlichen Präsentation des Selbst. Heiratsinserate von 1900 bis 2000. Pp. 75-107 in Bettina Heintz (ed.): 2001: *Geschlechtersoziologie*. Opladen: Westdeutscher Verlag.

Burkhart, Günter, 1993: Individualisierung und Elternschaft - Das Beispiel USA, in: *Zeitschrift für Soziologie* 22: 159-177.

Burkhart, Günter, 1998: Individualisierung und Elternschaft. Eine empirische Überprüfung der Individualisierungsthese am Beispiel USA und ein Systematisierungsvorschlag. Pp. 107–141 in: Jürgen Friedrichs (ed.), *Die Individualisierungsthese*. Opladen: Leske und Budrich.

Busch, Norbert, 1995: Die Feminisierung der ultramontanen Frömmigkeit. Pp. 203 – 220 in: Irmtraud Götz von Olenhusen (ed.), *Wunderbare Erscheinungen: Frauen und katholische Frömmigkeit im 19. und 20. Jahrhundert*. Paderborn u.a.: Schöningh.

Cerulo, Karen A., 1997: Identity Construction. New Issues, New Directions, in: *Annual Review of Sociology* 23: 385-409.

Chadwick, Bruce, Madeleine Gauthier, Louis Hourmant and Barbara Wörndl, 1994: Trends in Religion and Secularization. Pp. 173-214 in: Langlois, Simon (ed.), *Convergence or Divergence? Comparing Recent Social Trends in Industrial Societies*. Frankfurt a. M.: Campus.

Clark, Terry Nicolas, Lipset, Seymour Martin and Rempel, Michael, 1993: The declining political significance of social class, in: *International Sociology* 8: 293-316.

Coester, Michael, 1986: Vornamensrecht – international. Pp. 5-17 in: Gesellschaft für Deutsche Sprache und Bundesverband der deutschen Standesbeamten (ed.):

Internationales Handbuch der Vornamen. Frankfurt a. M.: Verlag für Standesamtswesen.

Coleman, James S., 1995: *Grundlagen der Sozialtheorie*, Vol. 1: *Handlungen und Handlungssysteme*. München/Wien: R. Oldenbourg.

Conradt, David, 1980: Changing German Political Culture. Pp. 212-272 in: Gabriel Almond and Sidney S. Verba (eds.): *The Civic Culture Revisited*. Boston: Sage.

Dahrendorf, Ralf, 1992: Der moderne soziale Konflikt. Stuttgart: Deutsche Verlags-Anstalt.

Daiber, Karl-Fritz, 1988: Kirche und religiöse Gemeinschaften in der DDR, in: *Gegenwartskunde. Sonderheft* 5: 75-88.

Daniel, Ute, 2001: *Kompendium Kulturgeschichte. Theorien, Praxis, Schlüsselwörter*. Frankfurt: Suhrkamp.

Dann, Otto, 1996: *Nation und Nationalismus in Deutschland. 1770-1990*, third edition. München : Beck.

Debus, Friedhelm, 1968: Soziologische Namengeographie. Zur sprachgeographisch-soziologischen Betrachtung der nomina propria. Pp. 315-338 in: Friedhelm Debus and Wilfried Seibicke, (1989): Reader zur Namenkunde I: Namentheorie. Hildesheim/Zürich/New York: Georg Olms Verlag.

Debus, Friedhelm, 1995: Soziolinguistik der Eigennamen. Name und Gesellschaft (Sozio-Onomastik). Pp. 393-399 in: Ernst Eichler, Gerold Hilty, Heinrich Löffler, Hugo Steeger, and Ladislav Zgusta (eds.), *Namensforschung: Ein internationales Handbuch der Onomastik*, Vol. 1. Berlin/New York: de Gruyter.

Debus, Friedhelm, 1996: Personennamen und soziale Schichtung. Pp. 1732-1738 in: Eichler, Ernst, Gerold Hilty and Heinrich Löffler (Hg): *Namenforschung. Ein internationales Handbuch zur Onomastik*, Vol. 2. Berlin: de Gruyter.

Debus, Friedhelm, 1996a: Methoden und Probleme der soziologisch orientierten Namenforschung. Pp. 344-351 in: Ernst Eichler, Gerold Hilty, Heinrich Löffler, Hugo Steger, and Ladislav Zgusta (eds.), *Namenforschung: ein internationales Handbuch zur Onomastik*, Vol. 2. Berlin/New York: de Gruyter.

Debus, Friedhelm, 1996b: Soziolinguistik der Eigennamen. Name und Gesellschaft (Sozio-Onomastik). Pp. 393-399 in: Ernst Eichler, Gerold Hilty, Heinrich Löffler, Hugo Steger and Ladislav Zgusta (Hg), *Namenforschung: Ein internationales Handbuch zur Onomastik*, Vol. 2. Berlin/New York: de Gruyter.

Debus, Friedhelm, Joachim Hartig, Hubertus Menke and Günter Schmitz, 1973: Namengebung und soziale Schicht. Bericht über ein Projekt zur Personennamenkunde, in: *Naamkunde* 5 : 368-405.

Debus, Friedhelm and Wilfried Seibicke, 1989: *Reader zur Namenkunde*, Bd. 1: *Namentheorie*. Hildesheim.

Desplanques, Guy, 1986: Les enfants de Michel et Martine Dupont s'appelent Nicolas et Céline, in: *Economie et Statistique* 184: 63-83.

Deutsch, Karl W., 1956: Shifts in the Balance of Communication Flows: A Problem of Measurement in International Relations, in: *Public Opinion Quarterly* 20: 143-160.

Diedrichsen, Uwe, 1996: Namensrecht, Namenspolitik. Pp. 1763-1780 in: Ernst Eichler u.a. (ed.): *Namenforschung. Ein internationales Handbuch zur Onomastik*, Bd. 2. Berlin: de Gruyter.

Diewald, Martin, 1991: *Soziale Beziehungen: Verlust oder Liberalisierung? Soziale Unterstützung in informellen Netzwerken.*, Berlin: Edition Sigma.

Doering-Manteuffel, Sabine, 1995: *Die Eifel. Geschichte einer Landschaft*. Frankfurt a. M./New York: Campus.

Drosdowski, Günther, 1974: *Duden Lexikon der Vornamen. Herkunft, Bedeutung und Gebrauch von mehreren tausend Vornamen*. Mannheim/Wien/Zürich: Dudenverlag.

Dupaquier, Jacques, 1981: Naming-Practices, Godparenthood, and Kindship in the Vexin, 1540-1900, in: *Journal of Family History* 6: 135-155.

Dupaquier, Jacques, Alain Biedeau, and Marie-Elizabeth Ducreux, 1984: *Le prénom: mode et histoire. Entretiens de Malher 1980*. Paris: Ecole des Hautes Etudes en Sciences Sociales.

Durkheim, Emile, 1895/1976: *Die Regeln der soziologischen Methode*. Herausgegeben von René König. Neuwied: Luchterhand (4. Auflage).

Durkheim, Emile, 1977: *Über die Teilung der sozialen Arbeit*. Frankfurt a. M.: Suhrkamp.

Durkheim, Emile, 1897/1983: *Der Selbstmord*. Frankfurt a. M.: Suhrkamp.

Ebers, Nicola, 1995: *„Individualisierung." Georg Simmel – Norbert Elias – Ulrich Beck*. Würzburg: Königshausen und Neumann.

Eichler, Ernst, Gerold Hilty, Heinrich Löffler, Hugo Steeger, and Ladislav Zgusta (eds.), 1995: *Namenforschung: ein internationales Handbuch der Onomastik*, Vol. 1. Berlin/ New York: de Gruyter.

Eichler, Ernst, Gerold Hilty, Heinrich Löffler, Hugo Steeger and Ladislav Zgusta (eds.), 1996: *Namenforschung: ein internationales Handbuch der Onomastik*, Vol. 2. Berlin/ New York: de Gruyter.

Eliade, Mircea, 1957: *Das Heilige und das Profane*. Hamburg: Rowohlt.

Elias, Norbert, 2001: *Über den Prozeß der Zivilisation*. Frankfurt: Suhrkamp.

Engels, Friedrich, 1973: Herrn Eugen Dührings Umwälzung der Wissenschaft, in: Karl Marx and Friedrich Engels, *Werke*, Volume 20, Berlin: Dietz Verlag.

Esser, Hartmut, 1991: *Alltagshandeln und Verstehen. Zum Verhältnis von erklärender und verstehender Soziologie am Beispiel von Alfred Schütz und 'Rational Choice'*. Tübingen: Mohr.

Esser, Hartmut, 1996: *Soziologie. Allgemeine Grundlagen*. Frankfurt a. M./New York: Campus.

Ester, Peter, Loek Halman and Ruud der Moor, 1993: *The Individualizing Society. Value Change in Europe and North America*. Tilburg: Tilburg University Press.

Evans, P.B., Dietrich Rüschemeyer and Theda Skocpol (eds.), 1985: *Bringing the State Back In*. Cambridge/New York: Cambridge University Press.

Fahrenkrog, Rolf Ludwig, 1939: *Deutschen Kindern – Deutsche Namen*. Berlin. Fritsch.

Ferree, Myra Marx, William A. Gamson, Jürgen Gerhards, and Dieter Rucht, 2002: *Shaping the Abortion Discourse: Democracy and The Public Sphere in Germany and the United States*. New York: Cambridge University Press.

Finke, Roger and Rodney Stark, 1992: *The Churching of America: 1776-1990. Winners and Losers in our Religious Economy*. New Brunswick, NJ: Rutgers University Press.

Flora, Peter and Jens Alber, 1982: Modernization, Democratization, and the Development of Welfare States in Western Europe, in: Peter Flora and Arnold J. Heidenheimer (eds.), *The Development of Welfare States in Europe and America*. New Brunswick, NJ: Transaction Publishers.

Frank, Rainer, 1977: *Zur Frage einer schichtenspezifischen Personennamengebung. Namenkundliche Sammlung, Analyse und Motivuntersuchung über den Kreis und die Stadt Segeberg*. Neumünster: Wachholtz.

Friedrichs, Jürgen, 1998: *Die Individualisierungsthese*. Opladen: Leske und Budrich.

Früh, Werner, 1992: Analyse sprachlicher Daten. Zur konvergenten Entwicklung "quantitativer" und "qualitativer" Methoden. Pp. 59–89 in: Hoffmeyer-Zlotnik, Jürgen H. P. (ed.): *Analyse verbaler Daten. Über den Umgang mit qualitativen Daten*. Opladen: Westdeutscher Verlag.

Früh, Werner, 1991: *Inhaltsanalyse. Theorie und Praxis, 3. Auflage*. München: Ohlschläger

Frühwald, Wolfgang, Hans Robert Jauß, Reinhart Kosseleck, Jürgen Mittelstraß, and Burkhart Steinwachs, 1991: *Geisteswissenschaften heute. Eine Dankschrift*. Frankfurt: Suhrkamp.

Fuchs, Dieter, Jürgen Gerhards and Edeltraud Roller, 1993: Wir und die Anderen. Ethnozentrismus in den zwölf Ländern der europäischen Gemeinschaft, in: *Kölner Zeitschrift für Soziologie und Sozialpsychologie* 45: 238-253.

Gabriel, Karl, 1990: Von der vordergründigen zur hintergründigen Religiosität: Zur Entwicklung von Religion und Kirche in der Geschichte der Bundesrepublik. Pp. 255-277 in: Robert Hettlage (ed.), *Die Bundesrepublik. Eine historische Bilanz.* München: Beck.

Galling, Kurt (ed.), 1986: *Die Religion in Geschichte und Gegenwart. Handwörterbuch für Theologie und Religionswissenschaft,* Bd. 3 und 5. Tübingen: Mohr.

Gatterer, Michael (ed.), 1941: *Das Religionsbuch der Kirche. (Catechismus Romanus).* Zweiter Teil: *Von den Sakramenten.* Innsbruck und Leipzig: Rauch.

Gebesmair, Andreas, 2000: *Musik und Globalisierung. Zur Repertoireentwicklung der transnationalen Phonoindustrie unter besonderer Berücksichtigung des österreichsichen Musikmarktes.* Forschungsbericht des Instituts Mediacult. Wien.

Geißler, Rainer, 1996: Kein Abschied von Klasse und Schicht. Ideologische Gefahren der deutschen Sozialstrukturanalyse, in: Kölner *Zeitschrift für Soziologie und Sozialpsychologie* 48: 319-338.

Gerbner, Georg, 1973: Cultural Indicators: The Third Voice. Pp. 555-571 in: George Gerbner, Larry P. Gross and William H. Melody (eds.), *Communications Technology and Social Policy. Understanding the New "Cultural Revolution*s*."* New York: John Wiley.

Gerbner, George, 1969: Toward »Cultural Indicators«: The Analysis of Mass Mediated Public Message Systems, in: *AV Communication Review* 17: 137-148.

Gerhards, Jürgen and Astrid Melzer, 1996: Die Semantik von Todesanzeigen als Indikator für Säkularisierungsprozesse, in: *Zeitschrift für Soziologie* 25: 304-314.

Gerhards, Jürgen and Jörg Rössel, 1999: Zur Transnationalisierung der Gesellschaft der Bundesrepublik. Entwicklungen, Ursachen und mögliche Folgen für die europäische Integration, in: *Zeitschrift für Soziologie* 28: 325-344.

Gerhards, Jürgen and Rolf Hackenbroch, 1997: Kulturelle Modernisierung und die Entwicklung der Semantik von Vornamen, in: *Kölner Zeitschrift für Soziologie und Sozialpsychologie* 49: 410-439.

Gerhards, Jürgen and Rolf Hackenbroch, 2000: Trends and Causes of Cultural Modernization. An Empircal Study of First Names, in: *International Sociology* 15: 501-532.

Gerhards, Jürgen, 1999: Rezension von Michael Wollfsohn und Thomas Brechenmacher: Die Deutschen und ihre Vornamen. 200 Jahre Politik und öffentliche Meinung. München 1999, in: *Kölner Zeitschrift für Soziologie und Sozialpsychologie* 51: 774-775.

Gerr, Elke, 1985: *Das große Vornamenbuch.* München: Humboldt.

Geserick, Rolf, 1989: *40 Jahre Presse, Rundfunk- und Kommunikationspolitik in der DDR.* München: Minerva.

Goffman, Erving, 1977: The Arrangment between the Sexes, in: *Theory and Society* 4: 301-331.

Goffman, Erving, 1979: *Gender Advertisments.* London: Macmillan.

Granger, C. W. J. and Newbold, P., 1974: Spurious Regressions in Econometrics, in: *Journal of Econometrics* 2: 111-120.

Grethlein, Christian, 1994: Name/Namengebung – IV. Kirchengeschichtlich. S 754-758 in: Gerhard Müller (ed.): *Theologische Realenzyklopädie.* Berlin/New York: de Gruyter.

Grethlein, Christian, 1994a: Name/Namengebung – V. Praktisch-theologisch. Pp. 758-760 in: Gerhard Müller (ed.), *Theologische Realenzyklopädie.* Berlin/New York: de Gruyter.

Grümer, Karl-Wilhelm and Robert Helmrich, 1994: Die Todesanzeige. Viel gelesen, jedoch wenig bekannt. Deskription eines wenig erschlossenen Forschungsmaterials, in: *Zeitschrift für Historische Sozialforschung* 19: 60-108.

Gugutschkow, Sabine and Karlheinz Hengst, 1998/1999: Vornamengebung in Deutschland und interkulturelle Kontakte. Beobachtungen zu Tendenzen in der gegenwärtigen Vornamenwahl, in: *Onoma. Journal of the International Council of Onomastic Sciences* 34.

Hahn, Alois, 1974: *Religion und der Weltverlust der Sinngebung. Identitätsprobleme in der modernen Gesellschaft.* Frankfurt am Main/New York: Campus.

Hannerz, Ulf, 1992: *Cultural Complexity. Studies in the Social Organization of Meaning.* New York: Columbia University Press.

Hausberger, Karl, 1994: Anfänge der christlichen Heiligenverehrung. Pp. 646-651 in: *Theologische Realenzyklopädie.* Berlin. De Gruyter.

Hausberger, Karl, 1994a: Heilige/Heiligenverehrung – Die römisch-katholische Kirche. Pp. 654-660 in: *Theologische Realenzyklopädie.* Berlin. De Gruyter.

Heckhausen, Heinz, 1989: *Motivation und Handeln*: Berlin: Springer (2. Auflage).

Heintz, Bettina, (ed.): 2001: *Geschlechtersoziologie.* Opladen: Westdeutscher Verlag.

Hengst, Karlheinz, 1999: Tendenzen in der Vornamengebung, in: *Der Sprachdienst* 43: 100-104.

Hirschauer, Stefan, 1989: Die interaktive Konstruktion von Geschlechtszugehörigkeit, in: *Zeitschrift für Soziologie* 18: 100-118.

Hirschfeld, Mattias, 2001: Transnationalisierung der Popmusikcharts in Deutschland 1960-2000. Unveröffentlichte Hausarbeit am Institut für Kulturwissenschaften der Universität Leipzig.

Hirschauer, Stefan, 1993: *Die soziale Konstruktion der Transsexualität. Über die Medizin und den Geschlechtswechsel.* Frankfurt: Suhrkamp.

Hitzler, Ronald and Anne Honer, 1995: Bastelexistenz. Über subjektive Konsequenzen der Individualisierung. Pp. 307-315 in: Ulrich Beck and Elisabeth Beck-Gernsheim (eds.): *Riskante Freiheiten.* Frankfurt a. M.: Suhrkamp.

Hobsbawm, Eric J. (ed.) 1984: *The Invention of Tradition.* Cambridge: Cambridge University Press.

Hohls, Rüdiger and Hartmut Kaeble, 1989: *Die regionale Erwerbsstruktur im Deutschen Reich und in der Bundesrepublik 1895-1970.* St. Katharinen: Scripta Mercaturae.

Hohorst, Gerd, Jürgen Kocka and Gerhard A. Ritter, 1975: *Sozialgeschichtliches Arbeitsbuch. Materialien zur Statistik des Kaiserreichs 1870-1914.* München: Beck.

Homann, Harald, 1994: Religion. Pp. 260-267 in: Siegfried Rudolf Dunde (ed.), *Wörterbuch der Religionssoziologie.* Gütersloh: Gütersloher Verlagshaus.

Horkheimer, Max and Theodor W. Adorno, 1978: Kulturindustrie. Aufklärung als Massenbetrug. Pp.108-150 in: Max Horkheimer and Theodor W. Adorno (eds.), *Dialektik der Aufklärung. Philosophische Fragmente.* Frankfurt a. M.: Fischer.

Hornborstel, Stefan, 1997: Eigennamen – die Politik der feinen Unterschiede. Pp. 407-414 in: Karl-Siegbert Rehberg (ed.), *Differenz und Integration. Die Zukunft moderner Gesellschaften.* Verhandlungen des 28. Kongresses der Deutschen Gesellschaft für Soziologie im Oktober 1996 in Dresden, Bd. 2. Opladen: Westdeutscher Verlag.

Hörsch, Nicoline, 1994: *Republikanische Personennamen. Eine anthroponymische Studie zur Französischen Revolution.* Tübingen: Niemeyer.

Huinink, Johannes and Michael Wagner, 1998: Individualisierung und die Pluralisierung von Lebensformen. Pp. 85-106 in: Jürgen Friedrichs (ed.), *Die Individualisierungsthese.* Opladen: Leske und Budrich.

Huinink, Johannes, Karl Ulrich Mayer and Michael Wagner, 1989: Ehe und Familie im Wandel der Nachkriegszeit — ein kritischer Beitrag zur aktuellen Diskussion. Pp. 66-68 in: Hans-Joachim Hoffmann-Nowotny (ed.), Kultur und Gesellschaft. Gemeinsamer Kongreß der Deutschen, Österreichischen und Schweizerischen Gesellschaft für Soziologie. Beiträge der Sektions- und Ad-hoc-Gruppen. Zürich: Seismo.

Imhof, Arthur E., 1994: Die neuen Überlebenden: Gestern – heute – morgen, in Deutschland, Europa, weltweit. Pp. 25-113 in: Arthur E. Imhof (ed.), *Lebenserwartungen in Deutschland, Norwegen und Schweden im 19. und 20. Jahrhundert.* Berlin: Akademie Verlag.

Inglehart, Ronald, 1989: *Kultureller Umbruch. Wertwandel in der westlichen Welt.* Frankfurt a. M./New York: Campus.

Jagodzinski, Wolfgang and Karel Dobbelaere, 1995: Secularization and Church Religiosity. Pp. 76-119 in: Jan W.van Deth and Elinoar Scarbrough (eds.), *The Impact of Values. Beliefs in Government,* Vol. 4. Oxford: Oxford University Press.

Jagodzinski, Wolfgang, 1995: Säkularisierung und religiöser Glaube. Rückgang traditioneller Religiösität und religiöser Pluralismus in Westeuropa. Pp. 261-285 in: Karl-Heinz Reuband, Fran Urban Pappi and Heinrich Best (eds.), *Die deutsche Gesellschaft in vergleichender Perspektive. Festschrift für Erwin K. Scheuch zum 65. Geburtstag.* Opladen: Westdeutscher Verlag.

Junge, Matthias, 1997: Georgs Simmels Individualisierungstheorie. Eine systematische Rekonstruktion ihrer Argumentationsfiguren, in: *Sociologia Internationalis* 35: 1-27.

Junge, Matthias, 2002: *Individualisierung.* Frankfurt: Campus.

Khatib, Syed-Malik, 1995: Personal Names and Name Changes, in: *Journal of Black Studies* 25: 349-353.

Kippele, Flavia, 1998: *Was heisst Individualisierung? Die Antworten soziologischer Klassiker.* Opladen: Westdeutscher Verlag.

Kleinöder, Rudolf, 1996: *Konfessionelle Namengebung in der Oberpfalz von der Reformation bis zur Gegenwart.* Frankfurt M.: Lang.

Kleinteich, Bernd, 1992: *Vornamen in der DDR 1960-1990.* Berlin. Akademie Verlag.

Knorr Cetina, Karin, 1988: Kulturanalyse: Ein Programm. Pp. 27-31 in: Hans Georg Soeffner (ed.), *Kultur und Alltag.* Göttingen: Otto Schwarz .

Kohlheim, Volker, 1988: Zur Verbreitung sprachlicher und onomastischer Neuerungen, in: *Beiträge zur Namensforschung. Neue Folge* 23: 158-176.

Kohlheim, Volker, 1996: Die christliche Namengebung. Pp. 1048-1057 in: Ernst Eichler, Gerold Hilty, Heinrich Löffler, Hugo Steger und Ladislav Zgusta (eds.), *Namenforschung: Ein internationales Handbuch zur Onomastik,* Vol. 2. Berlin/New York: de Gruyter.

Koß, Gerhard, 1990: *Namenforschung. Eine Einführung in die Onomastik.* Tübingen: Niemeyer.

Kristlieb, Adlof, 1994: Name/Namengebung – VI. Systematisch-theologisch. In: Gerhard Müller (ed.): *Theologische Realenzyklopädie.* Berlin/New York: de Gruyter.

Kron, Thomas (ed.), 2000: *Individualisierung und soziologische Theorie.* Opladen: Leske und Budrich.

Kunze, Konrad, 1998: *Namenkunde. Vor- und Familiennamen im deutschen Sprachgebiet.* München: dtv.

Lawson, Edwin D., 1984: Personal Names: 100 Years of Social Science Contributions, in: *Names - Journal of the American Name Society* 32: 45-73.

Lemm, Kristi and Mahzarin R. Banaji, 1999: Unconscious attitudes and beliefs about woman and men. Pp. 215-235 in: Ursula Pasero and Friederike Braun (eds.), *Wahrnehmung und Herstellung von Geschlecht.* Opladen: Westdeutscher Verlag.

Lenz, Karl and Lothar Bönisch, 1997: Zugänge zu Familien – ein Grundlagentext. Pp. 9-64 in: Lothar Bönisch and Karl Lenz (eds.), *Familien. Eine interdisziplinäre Einführung.* Weinheim und München: Juventa.

Lepsius, M. Rainer, 1989: Das Erbe des Nationalsozialismus und die politische Kultur der Nachfolgestaaten des 'Großdeutschen Reiches'. Pp. 247-264 in: Max Haller, Hans-Joachim Hoffmann-Nowotny and Wolfgang Zapf (eds.), Kultur und Gesellschaft. Verhandlungen des 24. Deutschen Soziologentags, des. 11. Österreichischen Soziologentags und des 8. Kongresses der Schweizerischen Gesellschaft für Soziologie in Zürich 1988. Frankfurt/M.: Campus.

Lévi-Strauss, Claude, 1968: *Das wilde Denken.* Frankfurt: Suhrkamp.

Lieberson, Stanley and Mikelson, Kelly S., 1995: Distinctive, African American Names: An Experimental, Historicial, And Linguistic Analysis of Innovation, in: *American Sociological Review* 60: 928-946.

Lieberson, Stanley, 1969: Measuring Population Diversity, in: *American Sociological Review* 34: 850-862.

Lieberson, Stanley, 1984: What´s in a name? ... some sociolinguistic possibilities, in: *International Journal of the Sociology of Language* 45: 77-87.

Lieberson, Stanley, 2000: *A Matter of Taste. How Names, Fashions, and Culture Change.* New Haven and London: Yale University Press.

Lieberson, Stanley and Eleanor O. Bell, 1992: Children´s First Names: An Empirical Study of Social Taste, in: *American Journal of Sociology* 98: 511-554.

Lieberson, Stanley, Susan Dumais and Shyon Baumann, 2000: The Instability of Androgynous Names: The Symbolic Maintenance of Gender Boundaries, in: *American Journal of Sociology* 105: 1249-1287.

Lindenberg, Siegwart, 1983: Zur Kritik an Durkheims Programm der Soziologie, in: *Zeitschrift für Soziologie* 12: 139-151.

Linke, Norbert, 1987: Die Rezeption der Programme von ARD und ZDF in der DDR als Gegenstand der SED-Kommunikationspolitik, in: *Publizistik* 32: 45-68.

Liwak, Rüdiger, 1994: Name/Namengebung – III. Biblisch, in: Gerhard Müller (ed.): *Theologische Realenzyklopädie.* Berlin/New York: de Gruyter.

London, Andrew S. and S. Philip Morgan, 1994: Racial Differences in First Names in 1910, in: *Journal of Family History* 19: 261-284.

Loos, Wolfgang, 1996: *Namensänderungsgesetz.* Neuwied: Luchterhand.

Lübbe, Hermann, 1965: *Säkularisierung – Geschichte eines ideenpolitischen Begriffs.* Freiburg: Alber.

Lukes, Steven, 1973: *Emile Durkheim. His Life and Work. A Historical and Critical Study.* London: Penguin.

Luckmann, Thomas, 1980a: Säkularisierung – ein moderner Mythos. Pp. 161-172 in: Thomas Luckmann: *Lebenswelt und Gesellschaft. Grundstrukturen und geschichtliche Wandlungen.* Paderborn u. a.: Schöningh.

Luckmann, Thomas, 1991: *Die unsichtbare Religion.* Frankfurt: Suhrkamp.

Luhmann, Niklas, 1977: *Funktion der Religion.* Frankfurt a. M.: Suhrkamp.

Luhmann, Niklas, 1981: Unverständliche Wissenschaft. Pp. 170–197 in Niklas Luhmann, *Soziologische Aufklärung,* Vol. 3. Opladen: Westdeutscher Verlag.

Luhmann, Niklas, 1984: *Soziale Systeme. Grundriß einer allgemeinen Theorie.* Frankfurt a. M.: Suhrkamp.

Main, Gloria L., 1996: Naming Children in Early New England, in: *Journal of Interdisciplinary History* 18: 1-27.

Martindale, Colin, 1990: *The Clockwork Muse. The Predictability of Artistic Change.* New York: Baisc Books.

Marx, Karl, 1972: Zur Kritik der Hegelschen Rechtsphilosophie (Einleitung), in: Karl Marx/ and Friedrich Engels, *Werke,* Vol. 1, Berlin: Dietz Verlag,.

Masser, Achim, 1992: *Tradition und Wandel. Studien zur Rufnamengebung in Südtirol.* Heidelberg.

Mayer, Karl Ulrich and Hans-Peter Blossfeld, 1990: Die gesellschaftliche Konstruktion sozialer Ungleichheit im Lebensverlauf. Pp. 297-318 in: Peter A. Berger and Stefan Hradil (eds.): *Lebenslagen, Lebensläufe, Lebensstile. Soziale Welt,* Sonderband 7. Göttingen: Otto Schwartz.

Mayer, Karl Ulrich and Walter Müller, 1987: Individualisierung und Standardisierung im Strukturwandel der Moderne. Lebensläufe im Wohlfahrtsstaat. Pp. 41-60 in: Ansgar Weymann (ed.): *Handlungsspielraum. Untersuchungen zur Individualisierung und Institutionalisierung von Lebensverläufen in der Moderne.* Stuttgart: Enke.

Mayer, Karl Ulrich, 1989: Empirische Sozialstrukturanalyse und Theorien gesellschaftlicher Entwicklung, in: *Soziale Welt* 40: 297-308.

McLeod, Hugh, 1988: Weibliche Frömmigkeit – männlicher Unglaube? Religion und Kirchen im bürgerlichen 19. Jahrhundert. Pp. 134-156 in: Ute Frevert (ed.), *Bürgerinnen und Bürger. Geschlechterverhältnisse im 19. Jahrhundert*. Göttingen: Vandenhoeck und Ruprecht.

Melischek, Gabriele, Karl Erik Rosengren and James Stappers (eds.), 1984: *Cultural Indicators: An International Symposium*. Wien: Verlag der österreichischen Akademie der Wissenschaften.

Merton, Robert K., 1968: *Social Theory and Social Structure*. New York and London: The Free Press.

Meulemann, Heiner, 1985: Wertewandel zwischen 1950 und 1980: Versuch einer zusammenfassenden Deutung vorliegender Zeitreihen. Pp. 391-411 in: Dieter Oberndörfer, Hans Rattinger and Karl Schmidt, 1985, Wirtschaftlicher Wandel, religiöser Wandel und Wertewandel. Folgen für das politische Verhalten in der Bundesrepublik Deutschland. Berlin: Dunker und Humblot.

Meulemann, Heiner, 1993: Säkularisierung und Werte. Eine systematische Übersicht über Ergebnisse aus Bevölkerungsumfragen in westeuropäischen Gesellschaften. Pp. 627-635 in: Bernhard Schäfers (ed.), Lebensverhältnisse und soziale Konflikte im neuen Europa. 26. Deutscher Soziologentag 1992. Plenarveranstaltungen. Frankfurt a. M.: Campus.

Miller, Nathan, 1927: Some Aspects of the Name in Culture-History, in: American Journal of Sociology *32: 585-600.*

Mitterauer, Michael, 1988: Namengebung, in: *Beiträge zur historischen Sozialkunde* 18: 36-70.

Mitterauer, Michael, 1989: Entwicklungstrends der Familie in der europäischen Neuzeit. Pp.179-194 in: Rosemarie Nave-Herz and Manfred Markefka (eds.), *Handbuch der Familien- und Jugendforschung*, Vol. 1: *Familienforschung*. Neuwied: Luchterhand.

Mitterauer, Michael, 1993: *Ahnen und Heilige. Namengebung in der europäischen Geschichte*. München: Beck.

Mosse, Goerge L., 1997: *Das Bild des Mannes. Zur Konstruktion der modernen Männlichkeit*. Stuttgart: Fischer.

Müller, Hans-Peter, 1993: Soziale Differenzierung und Individualität. Georg Simmels Gesellschafts- und Zeitdiagnose, in: *Berliner Journal für Soziologie* 3: 127-140.

Müller, Walter, 1997: Sozialstruktur und Wahlverhalten. Eine Widerrede gegen die Individualisierungsthese, in: *Kölner Zeitschrift für Soziologie und Sozialpsychologie* 49: 747-760.

Namenwirth, J. and Robert Philip Weber, 1987: *Dynamics of Culture*. Boston and London: Allen & Unwin.

Nassehi, Armin and Georg Weber, 1989: *Tod, Modernität und Gesellschaft. Entwurf einer Theorie der Todesverdrängung*. Opladen: Westdeutscher Verlag.

Naumann, Horst, 1973: Entwicklungstendenzen in der Rufnamengebung der Deutschen Demokratischen Republik, in: *Der Name in Sprache und Gesellschaft. Beiträge zur Theorie der Onomastik. Deutsch-slawische Forschungen zur Namenkunde und Siedlungsgeschichte* 27: 147-191.

Naumann, Horst, 1989: Soziolinguistische Aspekte der Onomastik. Pp. 391-397 in: Friedhelm Debus and Wilfried Seibicke 1989: *Reader zur Namenkunde* I: *Namentheorie*. Hildesheim/Zürich/New York: Georg Olms Verlag.

Naumann, Horst, Gerhard Schlimpert, and Johannes Schultheis, 1986: *Vornamen Heute*. Leipzig: Bibliographisches Institut.

Nave-Herz, Rosemarie and Corinna Omen-Isemann, 2001: Familie. Pp. 289-310 in: Hans Joas (ed.), *Lehrbuch der Soziologie*. Frankfurt: Campus

Neidhardt, Friedhelm, 1975: *Die Familie in Deutschland. Gesellschaftliche Stellung, Struktur und Funktion.* Opladen: Leske und Budrich.

Nowak, Kurt, 1995: Historische Wurzeln der Entkirchlichung in der DDR. Pp. 665 - 669 in: Heinz Sahner and Stefan Schwendtner (eds.), 27. Kongreß der Deutschen Gesellschaft für Soziologie. Gesellschaften im Umbruch. Sektionen und Arbeitsgruppen. Opladen: Westdeutscher Verlag.

Nowatschin, Alois, 1986: Die höhere Knabenschule in Gerolstein von 1911 bis 1953. Pp. 133-149 in: Stadt Gerolstein (ed.), *Gerolstein:* Gerolstein.

Nunner-Winkler, Gertrud, 1985: Identität und Individualität, in: *Soziale Welt* 36:466-482.

Nunner-Winkler, Gertrud, 2001: Geschlecht und Gesellschaft. Pp. 265-288 in: Hans Joas (ed.), *Lehrbuch der Soziologie.* Frankfurt a. M.: Campus.

von Olenhusen, Irmtraud Götz, 1995: Die Feminisierung von Religion und Kirche im 19. und 20. Jahrhundert: Forschungsstand und Forschungsperspektiven (Einleitung). Pp. 9-21 in: Irmtraud Götz von Olenhusen u.a. *Frauen unter dem Patriarchat der Kirchen. Katholikinnen und Protestantinnen im 19. und 20. Jahrundert.* Stuttgart u.a.: Kohlhammer.

Pasero, Ursula and Friederike Braun (eds.), 1999: *Wahrnehmung und Herstellung von Geschlecht.* Opladen: Westdeutscher Verlag.

Peters, Jan, Albert Felling and P. Scheepers, 1993: Individualisierung und Säkularisierung in den Niederlanden in den achtziger Jahren. Pp. 636-645 in: Bernhard Schäfers (ed.): Lebensverhältnisse und soziale Konflikte im neuen Europa. 26. Deutscher Soziologentag 199. Plenarveranstaltungen. Frankfurt a. M.: Campus.

Petzina, Dietmar, Werner Sbelshauser and Anselm Faust, 1978: *Sozialgeschichtliches Arbeitsbuch III: Materialien zur Statistik des Deutschen Reiches 1914 – 1945.* München: Beck.

Pierenkemper, Toni, 1987: The Standard of Living and Employment in Germany, 1850-1980: An Overview, in: *The Journal of European Economic History* 16: 51-73.

Pindyck, Robert S. and Rubinfeld, Daniel L., 1991: *Econometric Models and Economic Forecasts*, New York: McGraw Hill.

Popper, Karl R. , 1976: *Logik der Forschung.* Tübingen: Mohr.

Rabinow, Paul and William M. Sullivan (eds.) 1979: *Interpretive Social Science. A Second Look.* Berkeley: California University Press.

Raschauer, Bernhard, 1978: *Namensrecht.* Wien: Springer.

Reckwitz, Andreas, 1999: Praxis – Autopoiesis – Text. Pp. 19 – 49 in Reckwitz, Andreas and Holger Sievert (eds.), *Interpretation, Konstruktion, Kultur. Ein Paradigmenwechsel in den Sozialwissenschaften.* Opladen: Westdeutscher Verlag

Reckwitz, Andreas, 2000: *Die Transformation der Kulturtheorien. Zur Entwicklung eines Theorieprogramms.* Weilerswist: Velbrück.

Ritzer, George, 1998: *The McDonaldization Thesis: Explorations and Extensions.* London: Sage.

Robinson, William S., 1950: Ecological Correlations and the Behavior of Individuals, in: *American Sociological Review* 15: 351-357.

Rosengren, Karl Erik, 1981: Mass Communications as Cultural Indicators: Sweden, 1945-1975. Pp. 716-737 in: G. C. Wilhort and H. De Boek (eds.), *Mass Communication Review Yearbook 2.* Beverly Hills: Sage.

Rosengren, Karl Erik, 1986: Linking Culture and Other Societal Systems. Pp. 87-98 in: Ball-Rokeach and M. G. Cantor (eds.), *Media, Audience, and Social Structure.* Beverly Hills: Sage.

Rosengren, Karl Erik, 1989: Medienkultur: Forschungsansatz und Ergebnisse eines schwedische Langzeitprojekts, in: *Media Perspektiven* 6: 356-371.

Rossi, Alice S., 1965: Naming Children in Middle-Class Families, in: *American Sociological Review* 30: 499-513.

Rytlewski, Ralf and Manfred Opp des Hipt, 1987: *Die Bundesrepublik Deutschland in Zahlen. 1945/49 – 1980. Ein sozialgeschichtliches Arbeitsbuch.* München: Beck.

Sabean, David, 1998: *Kinship in Neckerhausen, 1700 – 1870.* Cambridge: Cambridge University Press.

Schimank, Uwe, 2000: Die individualisierte Gesellschaft – differenzierungs- und akteurstheoretisch betrachtet. Pp. 107-128 in: Thomas Kron (ed.), *Individualisierung und soziologische Theorie.* Opladen: Leske und Budrich.

Schneider, Irmela, 1990: *Film, Fernsehen & Co. Zur Entwicklung des Spielfilms in Kino und Fernsehen. Ein Überblick über Konzepte und Tendenzen.* Heidelberg: Carl Winter Universitätsverlag.

Schnell, Rainer and Ulrich Kohler, 1995: Empirische Untersuchung einer Individualisierungshypothese am Beispiel der Parteipräferenz von 1953-1992, in: *Kölner Zeitschrift für Soziologie und Sozialpsychologie* 47: 635-657.

Schnell, Rainer, Paul B. Hill, and Elke Esser, 1995: *Methoden der empirischen Sozialforschung.* München: Oldenbourg

Schroer, Markus, 2000: Negative, positive und ambivalente Individualisierung – erwartbare und überraschende Allianzen. Pp. 13-44 in Thomas Kron (ed.), *Individualisierung und soziologische Theorie.* Opladen: Leske und Budrich.

Schulz, Frieder, 1994: Heilige/Heiligenverehrung: Die protestantischen Kirchen. Pp. 664-672 in: *Theologische Realenzyklopädie.* Berlin: De Gruyter.

Schulze, Gerhard, 1992: *Die Erlebnisgesellschaft. Kultursoziologie der Gegenwart.* Frankfurt: Campus.

Seibert, Winfried, 1996: *Das Mädchen, das nicht Esther heißen durfte. Eine exemplarische Geschichte.* Leipzig: Reclam.

Seibicke, Wilfried, 1962: *Wie nennen wir unser Kind. Ein Vornamenbuch.* Lüneburg: Heiland-Verlag.

Seibicke, Wilfried, 1977: *Vornamen. Beihefte zur Muttersprache 2.* Wiesbaden.

Seibicke, Wilfried, 1977a: *Vornamen.* Wiesbaden: Verlag für deutsche Sprache.

Seibicke, Wilfried, 1991: *Vornamen. Zweite, vollständig überarbeitete Auflage.* Frankfurt: Verlag für Standesamtswesen.

Seibicke, Wilfried, 1996: Traditionen der Vornamengebung. Motivationen, Vorbilder, Moden: Germanisch. Pp. 1207-1214 in: Ernst Eichler, Gerold Hilty, Heinrich Löffler, Hugo Steger and Ladislav Zgusta (eds.), *Namenforschung: ein internationales Handbuch zur Onomastik,* Vol. 2. Berlin/New York: de Gruyter.

Seibicke, Wilfried, 1999: Vornamen und Kulturgeschichte. Pp. 59-68 in: Andreas Gardt, Ulrike Haß-Zumkehr and Thorsten Roelke (eds.), *Sprachgeschichte als Kulturgeschichte.* Berlin: de Gruyter.

Shin, Kwang Sook, 1980: *Schichtenspezifische Faktoren der Vornamengebung: empirische Untersuchung der 1961 und 1976 in Heidelberg vergebenen Vornamen.* Frankfurt a. M.: Lang.

Simmel, Georg, 1983/1908: *Soziologie. Untersuchungen über die Formen der Vergesellschaftung.* Berlin: Duncker und Humblot.

Simon, Michael, 1989: *Vornamen wozu? – Taufe, Patenwahl und Namengebung in Westfalen vom 17. Jahrhundert bis zum 20. Jahrhundert.* Münster: F. Coppenrath Verlag.

Simon, Michael, 1991: Der Pate als Namengeber, in: *Rheinisch-westfälische Zeitschrift für Volkskunde* 36: 215-227.

Skocpol, Theda, 1979: *States and Social Revolutions. A Comparative Analysis of France, Russia and China.* Cambridge and New York: Cambridge University Press.

Smart, Veronica, 1995: Personal Names in England. Pp. 782-786 in: Ernst Eichler, Gerold Hilty, Heinrich Löffler, Hugo Steger and Ladislav Zgusta (eds.), *Namenforschung: Ein internationales Handbuch zur Onomastik,* Vol 1. Berlin/New York: de Gruyter.

Smith, Daniel Scott, 1985: Child naming practices, kinship ties, and change in family attitudes in Hingham, Massachusetts, 1641-1880, in: *Journal of Social History* 18: 541-566.

Smudits, Alfred, 1998: Musik und Globalisierung: Die Phonographischen Industrien, Strukturen und Strategien, in: *Österreichische Zeitschrift für Soziologie* 23: 23-52.

Sperber, Jonathan, 1984: *Popular Catholicism in Nineteenth-Century Germany.* Princeton: Princeton University Press.

Spoenla-Metternich, Sebastian-Johannes von, 1997: *Namenserwerb, Namensführung und Namensänderung unter Berücksichtigung von Namensbestandteilen.* Frankfurt a. M.: Peter Lang.

Stadt Gerolstein (ed.), 1986: *Gerolstein*: Gerolstein.

Stadtverwaltung Grimma (ed.), 1999: *Grimma. Eine Lesebuch.* Radebeul: Edition Reintzsch.

Stark, Rodney, 2000: Die Religiosität der Deutschen und der Deutschamerikaner. Annäherung an ein „Experimentum Crucius." Pp. 111-126, in: Jürgen Gerhards (ed.), *Die Vermessung kultureller Unterschiede. USA und Deutschland im Vergleich.* Opladen: Westdeutscher Verlag.

Statistisches Bundesamt (ed.), 2000: *Datenreport 1999.* Bonn: Bundeszentrale für politische Bildung.

Stellmacher, Dieter, 1996: Namen und soziale Identität. Namentradition in Familien und Sippen. Pp. 1726-1731 in: Eichler, Ernst, Gerold Hilty, and Heinrich Löffler (eds.), *Namenforschung. Ein internationales Handbuch zur Onomastik*, Vol. 2. Berlin: de Gruyter.

Strand, Elizabeth A., 1999: Gender perception influences speech processing. Pp. 127-136 in: Ursula Pasero and Friederike Braun (eds.), *Wahrnehmung und Herstellung von Geschlecht.* Opladen: Westdeutscher Verlag.

Streiff-Fenart, Jocelyne, 1990: La nomination de l'enfant dans les familles franco-maghrebines, in : *Societes-Contemporaines* 4: 5-18.

Swaan, Abraham de, 1995: Die soziologische Untersuchung der transnationalen Gesellschaft, in: *Journal für Sozialforschung* 35: 107-120.

Taagepera, Rein and Ray, James Lee, 1977: A generalized index of concentration, in: *Sociological Methods & Research* 5: 367-384.

Taylor, Rex, 1974: John Doe, Jr.: A Study of his Distribution in Space, Time, and the Social Structure, in: *Social Forces* 53: 11-21.

Teiche, Jutta, 1999: Grimma als Garnison. Pp. 124 – 129 in Stadtverwaltung Grimma (ed.), *Grimma. Eine Lesebuch.* Radebeul: Edition Reintzsch.

Teiche, Jutta, 1999a: Grimmas Fabriken: Pp. 158-169 in Stadtverwaltung Grimma (ed.), *Grimma. Eine Lesebuch.* Radebeul: Edition Reintzsch..

Teiche, Jutta, Horst Naumann and G. Schwalbe, 1999: Der Weg zur Schulstadt. Pp. 82-101 in Stadtverwaltung Grimma (ed.), 1999: *Grimma. Eine Lesebuch.* Radebeul: Edition Reintzsch.

Tenbruck, Friedrich H., 1989: *Die kulturellen Grundlagen der Gesellschaft. Der Fall der Moderne.* Opladen: Westdeutscher Verlag.

Tenbruck, Friedrich H., 1990: Repräsentative Kultur. Pp. 20-53 in: Hans Haferkamp (ed.), *Sozialstruktur und Kultur.* Frankfurt a. M.: Suhrkamp.

Trautner, Hanns Martin, 1991: Lehrbuch der Entwicklungspsychologie, Vol. 2: *Theorien und Befunde.* Göttingen u.a.: Hogrefe.

Troeltsch, Ernst, 1961: *Die Soziallehren der christlichen Kirchen und Gruppen. Gesammelte Schriften.* Bd. 1, Aalen: Scientia.

Tyrell, Hartmann, 1986: Geschlechtliche Klassifizierung und Geschlechterklassifikation, in: *Kölner Zeitschrift für Soziologie und Sozialpsychologie* 38: 450-489.

Wagner, Michael, 1989: *Räumliche Mobilität im Lebensverlauf. Eine empirische Untersuchung der Bedingungen der Migration.* Stuttgart: Enke.

Wallmann, Johannes, 1985: *Kirchgeschichte Deutschlands seit der Reformation*, fifth edition. Tübingen: Mohr-Siebeck (UTB).

Walther, Hans, 1973: Gesellschaftliche Entwicklung und geschichtliche Entfaltung von Wortschatz und Namenschatz. Pp. 339-355 in: Friedhelm Debus and Wilfried Seibicke (eds.), *Reader zur Namenkunde* I: *Namentheorie*. Hildesheim/Zürich/New York: Georg Olms Verlag.

Watkins, Susan Cotts and London, Andrew S., 1994: Personal Names and Cultural Change. A Study of the Naming Patterns of Italians and Jews in the United States in 1910, in: *Social Science History* 18: 169-209.

Weber, Max, 1980: *Wirtschaft und Gesellschaft. Grundriß der verstehenden Soziologie*, fifth edition. Tübingen: Mohr.

Weber, Max, 1988: *Gesammelte Aufsätze zur Religionssoziologie* I. Tübingen: Mohr.

Wehler, Hans-Ulrich, 1987: *Deutsche Gesellschaftsgeschichte*, Vol. 1: *Vom Feudalismus des Alten Reiches bis zur Defensiven Modernisierung der Reformära 1700-1815*. München: Beck.

Wehler, Hans-Ulrich, 1987a: *Deutsche Gesellschaftsgeschichte*, Vol. 2: *Von der Reformära bis zur industriellen und politischen „Deutschen Doppelrevolution." 1815-1845/49*. München: Beck.

Wehler, Hans-Ulrich, 1995: *Deutsche Gesellschaftsgeschichte*, Vol. 3: *Von der „Deutschen Doppelrevolution" bis zum Beginn des Ersten Weltkriegs. 1849-1914*. München: Beck.

Weitman, Sasha, 1981: Some Methodological Issues in Quatitative Onomastics, in: *Names, Journal of the American Name Society* 29: 181-196.

Weitman, Sasha, 1982: Cohort Size and Onomasticon Size, in: *Onoma. Bibliographical and Information Bulletin* 26: 78-95.

Weitman, Sasha, 1987: Prénoms et orientations nationales en Israel, 1882-1980, in : *Annales* 42: 879-900.

West, Candice and Don H. Zimmermann, 1991: „Doing Gender." Pp. 13–37 in: Judith Lorber and Susan A. Farell (eds.), *The Social Construction of Gender*. Newbury Park: Sage.

Wicke, Peter, 1996: Die Charts im Musikgeschäft, in: Musik und Unterricht 40/96: 9-14.

Wilson, Stephen, 1998: *The Means of Naming. A Social and Cultural History of Personal Naming in Western Europe*. London: UCL Press.

Wohlrab-Sahr, Monika, 1997: Individualisierung: Differenzierungsprozess und Zurechnungsmodus. Pp. 23-36 in: Ulrich Beck and Peter Sopp (eds.), *Individualisierung und Integration. Neue Konfliktlinien und neuer Integrationsmodus*. Opladen: Leske und Budrich.

Wohlrab-Sahr, Monika, 2001: Säkularisierte Gesellschaft. Pp. 308-332 in: Georg Kneer, Armin Nassehi and Markus Schoer (eds.), *Klassische Gesellschaftsbegriffe der Soziologie*. München: Fink (UTB).

Wolffsohn, Michael, and Thomas Brechenmacher, 1992: Vornamen als demoskopischer Indikator? München 1785-1876, in: *Zeitschrift für bayerische Landesgeschichte* 55: 543-573.

Wolffsohn, Michael and Thomas Brechenmacher, 1999: *Die Deutschen und ihre Vornamen. 200 Jahre Politik und öffentliche Meinung*, München und Zürich: Diana.

Wolffsohn, Michael and Thomas Brechenmacher, 2000: Nomen est Omen. Vornamenwahl als demoskopischer Indikator – das Beispiel München (1787-1876), in: *Geschichte in Wissenschaft und Unterricht* 51: 313-332.

Zabel, Hermann, 1984: Säkularisation, Säkularisierung. Pp. 789-829 in: Otto Brunner, Werner Conze and Reinhart Kosseleck (eds.), *Geschichtliche Grundbegriffe. Historisches Lexikon zur politischen und sozialen Sprache in Deutschland*. Bd. 5. Stuttgart: Klett-Cotta.

Zürn, Michael, 1998: *Regieren jenseits des Nationalstaates. Globalisierung und Denationalisierung als Chance.* Frankfurt am Main: Suhrkamp.

Zurstiege, Guido, 1998: *Mannsbilder – Männlichkeit in der Werbung. Ein Untersuchung zur Darstellung von Männern in der Anzeigenwerbung der 50-er, 70-er und 90-er Jahre.* Opladen: Westdeutscher Verlag.

Zwahr, Hartmut, 1996: Der Distelfink unter der Pickelhaube. Namen, Symbole und Identitäten Geächteter. Pp. 325-334 in Hartmut Zwahr, *Revolutionen in Sachsen. Beiträge zur Sozial- und Kulturgeschichte.* Weimar u. a.: Böhlau Verlag.

Index